Great Battles of World War Two

Battle of Iwo Jima

Compiled by

Pandora Ruff

Scribbles

Year of Publication 2018

ISBN : 9789352979332

Book Published by

Scribbles

(An Imprint of Alpha Editions)

email - alphaedis@gmail.com

Produced by: PediaPress GmbH
Limburg an der Lahn
Germany
http://pediapress.com/

Contents

Introduction

Battle of Iwo Jima

Battle of Iwo Jima
Part of the Pacific Theatre of World War II

A U.S. 37 mm (1.5 in) gun fires against Japanese cave positions in the north face of Mount Suribachi.

Date	19 February – 26 March 1945
Location	Iwo Jima, Volcano Islands
Result	American victory

Belligerents	
United States	Japan

Commanders and leaders	
U.S. Navy: Chester W. Nimitz Raymond A. Spruance Marc A. Mitscher William H.P. Blandy U.S. Marine Corps: Holland M. Smith Harry Schmidt Graves B. Erskine Clifton B. Cates Keller E. Rockey	Tadamichi Kuribayashi † Takeichi Nishi † Senda Sadasue † Rinosuke Ichimaru †

Units Involved	
Ground units: 🛡 **V Amphibious Corps** • 3rd Marine Division • 4th Marine Division • 5th Marine Division • 147th Infantry Regiment (separate) *Aerial units*: 🌀 **Seventh Air Force** *Naval units*: 🌀 **U.S. 5th Fleet** • Joint Expeditionary Force (TF 51) • Amphibious Support Force (TF 52) • Attack Force (TF 53) • Expeditionary Troops (TF 56) • Fast Carrier Force (TF 58) *Additional naval, air and ground support elements*	*Ground units*: ※ **109th IJA Division** • Headquarters Group • 2nd Mixed Brigade • 3rd Battalion, 17th Mixed Regiment • 26th Tank Regiment • 145th Infantry Regiment • Brigade Artillery Group *Naval Units*: ※ **Imperial Navy** • Naval Guard Force (mainly AA and Art.) *Additional support units and Kamikaze*
Strength	
110,000 U.S. Marines, U.S. Soldiers, U.S. Navy corpsmen, USAAF personnel, and others 500+ ships	20,530–21,060 troops 23 tanks[1] 438 artillery pieces 33 naval guns 69 anti-tank guns ~300 anti-aircraft guns[2]
Casualties and losses	
26,040 total casualties 6,821 killed 2 captured but recovered 19,217 wounded 1 escort carrier sunk 1 fleet carrier severely damaged 1 escort carrier lightly damaged	17,845–18,375 dead and missing 216 taken prisoner ~3,000 in hiding[3]

The **Battle of Iwo Jima** (19 February – 26 March 1945) was a major battle in which the United States Marine Corps landed on and eventually captured the island of Iwo Jima from the Imperial Japanese Army (IJA) during World War II. The American invasion, designated *Operation Detachment*, had the goal of capturing the entire island, including the three Japanese-controlled airfields (including the South Field and the Central Field), to provide a staging area for attacks on the Japanese main islands. This five-week battle comprised some of the fiercest and bloodiest fighting of the Pacific War of World War II.

After the heavy losses incurred in the battle, the strategic value of the island became controversial. It was useless to the U.S. Army as a staging base and useless to the U.S. Navy as a fleet base. However, Navy Seabees rebuilt the landing strips, which were used as emergency landing strips for USAAF B-29s.

The IJA positions on the island were heavily fortified, with a dense network of bunkers, hidden artillery positions, and 18 km (11 mi) of underground tunnels. The American ground forces were supported by extensive naval artillery, and had complete air supremacy provided by U.S. Navy and Marine Corps aviators throughout the entire battle.

Japanese combat deaths numbered three times the number of American deaths although, uniquely among Pacific War Marine battles, American total casualties (dead and wounded) exceeded those of the Japanese. Of the 21,000 Japanese soldiers on Iwo Jima at the beginning of the battle, only 216 were taken prisoner, some of whom were captured because they had been knocked unconscious or otherwise disabled.[4] The majority of the remainder were killed in action, although it has been estimated that as many as 3,000 continued to resist within the various cave systems for many days afterwards, eventually succumbing to their injuries or surrendering weeks later.[5]

Despite the bloody fighting and severe casualties on both sides, the American victory was assured from the start. Overwhelming American superiority in numbers and arms as well as complete air supremacy—coupled with the impossibility of Japanese retreat or reinforcement, along with sparse food and supplies—permitted no plausible circumstance in which the Americans could have lost the battle.[6]

On February 19, 1945, the 133rd Naval Construction Battalion (NCB) joined the Fifth Marine Amphibious Corps and the Fourth Marine Division for the amphibious assault on Iwo Jima. The entire force landed on Iwo Jima on D-Day with the first assault wave led by the Fourth Marine Division. The 133rd NCHB suffered severe casualties during the fight for Iwo Jima, where it distinguished itself in both front-line combat and construction. The 133rd NCHC had 370 casualties, more than 40 percent of the 875 men that landed, the highest casualties as part of a single battle in Seabee history.

Joe Rosenthal's Associated Press photograph of the raising of the U.S. flag on top of the 169 m (554 ft) Mount Suribachi by six U.S. Marines became an iconic image of the battle and the American war effort in the Pacific.

Background

After the American capture of the Marshall Islands, and the devastating air attacks against the Japanese fortress island of Truk Atoll in the Carolines in January 1944, the Japanese military leaders reevaluated their situation. All indications pointed to an American drive toward the Mariana Islands and the

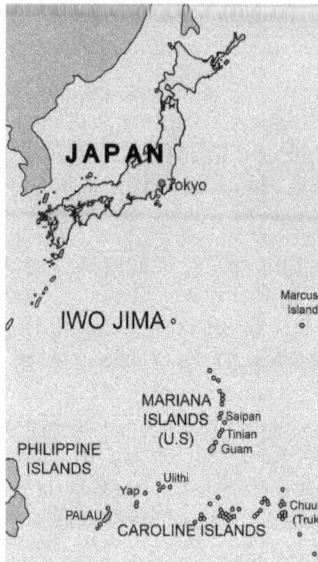

Figure 1: *Location of Iwo Jima*

Carolines. To counter such an offensive, the IJA and the Imperial Japanese Navy (IJN) established an inner line of defenses extending generally northward from the Carolines to the Marianas, and thence to Japan via the Volcano Islands, and westward from the Marianas via the Carolines and the Palau Islands to the Philippines.

In March 1944, the Japanese 31st Army, commanded by General Hideyoshi Obata, was activated to garrison this inner line. (Note that a Japanese army was about the size of an American, British Army, or Canadian Army corps. The Japanese Army had many armies, but the U.S. Army only had ten at its peak, with the 4th Army, the 6th Army, the 8th Army, and the 10th Army being in the Pacific Theater. Also, the 10th Army only fought on Okinawa in the spring of 1945.)

The commander of the Japanese garrison on Chichi Jima was placed nominally in command of Army and Navy units in the Volcano Islands. After the American conquest of the Marianas, daily bomber raids from the Marianas hit the mainland as part of Operation *Scavenger*. Iwo Jima served as an early warning station that radioed reports of incoming bombers back to mainland Japan. This allowed Japanese air defenses to prepare for the arrival of American bombers.

After the U.S. seized bases in the Marshall Islands in the battles of Kwajalein and Eniwetok in February 1944, Japanese Army and Navy reinforcements were sent to Iwo Jima: 500 men from the naval base at Yokosuka and 500 from Chichi Jima reached Iwo Jima during March and April 1944. At the same time, with reinforcements arriving from Chichi Jima and the home islands, the Army garrison on Iwo Jima reached a strength of more than 5,000 men. The loss of the Marianas during the summer of 1944 greatly increased the importance of the Volcano Islands for the Japanese, who were aware that the loss of these islands would facilitate American air raids against the Home Islands, disrupting war manufacturing and severely damaging civilian morale.

Final Japanese plans for the defense of the Volcano Islands were overshadowed by several factors:

1. the Imperial Japanese Navy had already lost almost all of its power, and it could not prevent American landings.
2. aircraft losses throughout 1944 had been so heavy that, even if war production were not affected by American air attacks, combined Japanese air strength was not expected to increase to 3,000 warplanes until March or April 1945.
3. these aircraft could not be used from bases in the Home Islands against Iwo Jima because their range was not more than 900 km (560 mi).
4. available warplanes had to be hoarded to defend Taiwan and the Japanese Home Islands from any attack.
5. there was a serious shortage of properly trained and experienced pilots and other aircrew to man the warplanes Japan had—because such large numbers of pilots and crewmen had perished fighting over the Solomon Islands and during the Battle of the Philippine Sea in mid-1944.

In a postwar study, Japanese staff officers described the strategy that was used in the defense of Iwo Jima in the following terms:

In the light of the above situation, seeing that it was impossible to conduct our air, sea, and ground/ operations on Iwo Island [Jima] toward ultimate victory, it was decided that to gain time necessary for the preparation of the Homeland defense, our forces should rely solely upon the established defensive equipment in that area, checking the enemy by delaying tactics. Even the suicidal attacks by small groups of our Army and Navy airplanes, the surprise attacks by our submarines, and the actions of parachute units, although effective, could be regarded only as a strategical ruse on our part. It was a most depressing thought that we had no available means left for the exploitation of the strategical opportunities which might from time to time occur in the course of these operations.[7]

—*Japanese Monograph No. 48*

At the end of the Battle of Leyte in the Philippines, the Allies were left with a two-month lull in their offensive operations before the planned invasion of

Okinawa. Iwo Jima was strategically important. It provided an air base for Japanese fighter planes to intercept long-range B-29 Superfortress bombers, and it provided a haven for Japanese naval units in dire need of any support available. In addition, it was used by the Japanese to stage air attacks on the Mariana Islands from November 1944 through January 1945. The capture of Iwo Jima would eliminate these problems and provide a staging area for Operation Downfall – the eventual invasion of the Japanese Home Islands. The distance of B-29 raids could (hypothetically) be cut in half, and a base would be available for P-51 Mustang fighters to escort and protect the bombers.

American intelligence sources were confident that Iwo Jima would fall in one week. In light of the optimistic intelligence reports, the decision was made to invade Iwo Jima and the operation was given the code name Operation *Detachment*. American forces were unaware that the Japanese were preparing a complex and deep defense, radically departing from their usual strategy of a beach defense. So successful was the Japanese preparation that it was discovered after the battle that the hundreds of tons of Allied bombs and thousands of rounds of heavy naval gunfire had left the Japanese defenders almost undamaged and ready to inflict losses on the U.S. Marines.

Planning and preparation

Japanese preparations

By June 1944, Lieutenant General Tadamichi Kuribayashi was assigned to command the defense of Iwo Jima. Kuribayashi knew that Japan could not win the battle, but he hoped to inflict massive casualties on the American forces, so that the United States and its Australian and British allies would reconsider carrying out the invasion of Japan Home Islands.

While drawing inspiration from the defense in the Battle of Peleliu, Kuribayashi designed a defense that broke with Japanese military doctrine. Rather than establishing his defenses on the beach to face the landings directly, he created strong, mutually supporting defenses in depth using static and heavy weapons such as heavy machine guns and artillery. Takeichi Nishi's armored tanks were to be used as camouflaged artillery positions. Because the tunnel linking the mountain to the main forces was never completed, Kuribayashi organized the southern area of the island in and around Mount Suribachi as a semi-independent sector, with his main defensive zone built up in the north. The expected American naval and air bombardment further prompted the creation of an extensive system of tunnels that connected the prepared positions, so that a pillbox that had been cleared could be reoccupied. This network of bunkers and pillboxes favored the defense. For instance, The Nanpo Bunker (Southern Area Islands Naval Air HQ), which was located east of Airfield

Figure 2: *Lieut. Gen. Tadamichi Kuribayashi*

Number 2, had enough food, water and ammo for the Japanese to hold out for three months. The bunker was 90 feet deep and had tunnels running in various directions. Approximately 500 55-gallon drums filled with water, kerosene, and fuel oil for generators were located inside the complex. Gasoline powered generators allowed for radios and lighting to be operated underground.

By February 19, 1945, the day the Americans invaded, 11 miles of a planned 17 miles of tunnel network had been dug. Besides the Nanpo Bunker, there were numerous command centers and barracks that were 75 feet deep. Tunnels allowed for troop movement to go undetected to various defense positions.

Hundreds of hidden artillery and mortar positions along with land mines were placed all over the island. Among the Japanese weapons were 320 mm spigot mortars and a variety of explosive rockets.

Nonetheless, the Japanese supply was inadequate. Troops were supplied 60% of the standard issue of ammunition sufficient for one engagement by one division, and food and forage for four months.[8]

Numerous Japanese snipers and camouflaged machine gun positions were also set up. Kuribayashi specially engineered the defenses so that every part of Iwo Jima was subject to Japanese defensive fire. He also received a handful of *kamikaze* pilots to use against the enemy fleet. Three hundred and eighteen American sailors were killed by *kamikaze* attacks during the battle. However, against his wishes, Kuribayashi's superiors on Honshu ordered him to erect some beach defenses. These were the only parts of the defenses that were destroyed during the pre-landing bombardment.

American preparations

Starting on 15 June 1944, the U.S. Navy and the U.S. Army Air Forces began naval bombardments and air raids against Iwo Jima, which would become the longest and most intense in the Pacific theater. These would contain a combination of naval artillery shellings and aerial bombings that went on for nine months. On 17 February, the destroyer escort USS *Blessman* sent Underwater Demolition Team 15 (UDT-15) toward Blue Beach for reconnaissance. The Japanese infantry fired on them, killing one American diver. On the evening of 18 February, the *Blessman* was hit by a bomb from a Japanese aircraft, killing 40 sailors, including 15 members of her UDT.

Unaware of Kuribayashi's tunnel defense system, many of the Americans assumed the majority of the Japanese garrison were killed by the constant bombing raids.

"Well, this will be easy. The Japanese will surrender Iwo Jima without a fight."
– Chester W. Nimitz

Pre-landing bombardment

Maj. Gen. Harry Schmidt, commander of the Marine landing force, requested a 10-day heavy shelling of the island immediately preceding the mid-February amphibious assault. However, Rear Adm. William H. P. Blandy, commander of the Amphibious Support Force (Task Force 52), did not believe such a bombardment would allow him time to replenish his ships' ammunition before the landings; he thus refused Schmidt's request. Schmidt then asked for nine days of shelling; Blandy again refused and agreed to a three-day bombardment. This decision left much hard feeling among the Marines. After the war, Lieut. Gen. Holland M. "Howlin' Mad" Smith, commander Expeditionary Troops (Task Force 56, which consisted of Schmidt's Fifth Amphibious Corps), bitterly complained that the lack of naval gunfire had cost Marine lives during the entire Allied island campaign.[9]

Each heavy warship was given an area on which to fire that, combined with all the ships, covered the entire island. Each warship fired for approximately six hours before stopping for a certain amount of time. Poor weather on D minus 3 led to uncertain results for that day's bombardment. On D minus 2, the time and care that the Japanese had taken in preparing their artillery positions became clear. When heavy cruiser USS *Pensacola* got within range of shore batteries, the ship was quickly hit 6 times and suffered 17 crew deaths.

Figure 3: *The battleship USS New York firing its 14 in (360 mm) main guns on the island, 16 February 1945 (D minus 3)*

Later, 12 small craft attempting to land an underwater demolition team were all struck by Japanese rounds and quickly retired. While aiding these vessels, the destroyer USS *Leutze* was also hit and suffered 7 crew deaths. On D minus 1, Adm. Blandy's gunners were once again hampered by rain and clouds. Gen. Schmidt summed up his feelings by saying, "We only got about 13 hours worth of fire support during the 34 hours of available daylight."[10]

The limited bombardment had questionable impact on the enemy due to the Japanese being heavily dug-in and fortified. However, many bunkers and caves were destroyed during the bombing, giving it some limited success. The Japanese had been preparing for this battle since March 1944, which gave them a significant head start. By the time of the landing, about 450 American ships were located off Iwo Jima. The entire battle involved about 60,000 U.S. Marines and several thousand U.S. Navy Seabees.

Lt. (jg) Rufus G. Herring, USNR received the Medal of Honor for his actions on D-Day minus 2.

Figure 4: *Maj. Gen. Harry Schmidt*

Opposing forces

General Schmidt's division commanders on Iwo Jima

Maj. Gen. Keller Rockey

Maj. Gen. Clifton Cates

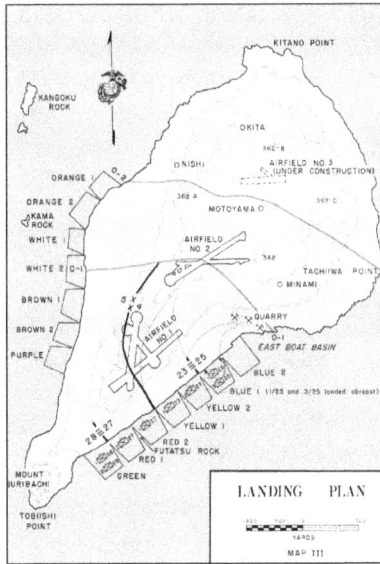

Figure 5: *Map of Iwo Jima detailing the invasion*

Maj. Gen. Graves Erskine

American order of battle

Joint Expeditionary Force (Task Force 51)
Vice Admiral R. Kelly Turner, commanding

- Amphibious Support Force (Task Force 52), Rear Admiral William H.P. Blandy
- Attack Force (Task Force 53), Rear Admiral Harry W. Hill
- Expeditionary Troops (Task Force 56), Lieut. Gen. Holland M. Smith, USMC

Fifth Amphibious Corps[11]

- Commanding General: Maj. Gen. Harry Schmidt, USMC
- Chief of Staff: Brig. Gen. William W. Rogers, USMC

- Personnel officer (G-1): Col. David A. Stafford, USMC
- Intelligence officer (G-2): Col. Thomas R. Yancey, USA
- Operations officer (G-3): Col. Edward A. Craig, USMC
- Logistics officer (G-4): Col. William F. Brown, USMC

Southern sector (Green and Red beaches):

- **5th Marine Division** (25,884 officers and enlisted)
- Division Commander: Maj. Gen. Keller E. Rockey
- Assistant Division Commander: Brig. Gen. Leo D. Hermle
- Chief of Staff: Col. Ray A. Robinson
    - 26th Marine Regiment: Col. Chester B. Graham
    - 27th Marine Regiment: Col. Thomas A. Wornham
    - 28th Marine Regiment: Col. Harry B. Liversedge
    - 13th (Artillery) Marine Regiment: Col. James D. Waller
    - 5th Tank Battalion: Lt. Col. William R. Collins

Northern sector (Yellow and Blue beaches):

- **4th Marine Division** (24,452 officers and enlisted)
- Division Commander: Maj. Gen. Clifton B. Cates
- Assistant Division Commander: Brig. Gen. Franklin A. Hart
- Chief of Staff: Col. Merton J. Batchelder
    - 23rd Marine Regiment: Col. Walter W. Wensinger
    - 24th Marine Regiment: Col. Walter I. Jordan
    - 25th Marine Regiment: Col. John R. Lanigan
    - 14th (Artillery) Marine Regiment: Col. Louis G. DeHaven

Floating reserve (committed to center sector 22 Feb):

- **3rd Marine Division** (19,597 officers and enlisted)
- Division Commander: Maj. Gen. Graves B. Erskine
- Assistant Division Commander: Brig. Gen. William A. Worton
- Chief of Staff: Col. Robert E. Hogaboom
    - 3rd Marine Regiment (Floating reserve): Col. James A. Stuart
    - 9th Marine Regiment: Col. Howard N. Kenyon
    - 21st Marine Regiment: Col. Hartnoll J. Withers
    - 12th (Artillery) Marine Regiment: Lt.Col. Raymond F. Crist Jr.

Japanese order of battle

21,060 total men under arms
Lieut. General Tadamichi Kuribayashi, commanding
Colonel Tadashi Takaishi, chief of staff
Army

- 109th Division

Figure 6: *LVTs approach Iwo Jima.*

- 145th Infantry Regiment
- 17th Mixed Infantry Regiment
- 26th Tank Regiment
- 2nd Mixed Brigade

Navy

- 125th Anti-Aircraft Defense Unit
- 132nd Anti-Aircraft Defense Unit
- 141st Anti-Aircraft Defense Unit
- 149th Anti-Aircraft Defense Unit

First day – 19 February 1945

Amphibious landing

During the night, Vice Adm. Marc A. Mitscher's Task Force 58, a huge carrier force, arrived off Iwo Jima. Also in this flotilla was Adm. Raymond A. Spruance, overall commander for the invasion, in his flagship, the heavy cruiser USS *Indianapolis*. "Howlin' Mad" Smith was once again deeply frustrated that Mitscher's powerful carrier group had been bombing the Japanese home islands instead of softening up the defenses of Iwo Jima. Mitscher's fliers did contribute to the additional surface-ship bombardment that accompanied the formation of the amphibious craft.[12]

Figure 7: *Marines landing on the beach*

Figure 8: *Members of the 1st Battalion 23rd Marines burrow in the volcanic sand on Yellow Beach 1. A beached LCI is visible upper left with Mount Suribachi upper right*

Unlike the days of the pre-landing bombardment, D-Day dawned clear and bright. At 08:59, one minute ahead of schedule, the first wave of Marines landed on the beaches of the southeastern coast of Iwo Jima. Major Howard Connor, 5th Marine Division signal officer, had six Navajo code talkers working around the clock during the first two days of the battle. These six sent and received over 800 messages, all without error. Connor later stated, "Were it not for the Navajos, the Marines would never have taken Iwo Jima."[13]

Situation on the beaches

Unfortunately for the landing force, the planners at Pearl Harbor had completely misjudged the situation that would face Gen. Schmidt's Marines. The beaches had been described as "excellent" and the thrust inland was expected to be "easy." In reality, after crossing the beach, the Marines were faced with 15-foot-high slopes of soft black volcanic ash.[14] This ash allowed for neither a secure footing nor the construction of foxholes to protect the Marines from hostile fire. However, the ash did help to absorb some of the fragments from Japanese artillery.

Marines were trained to move rapidly forward; here they could only plod. The weight and amount of equipment was a terrific hindrance and various items were rapidly discarded. First to go was the gas mask ...[14]

The lack of a vigorous response led the Navy to conclude that their bombardment had suppressed the Japanese defenses and in good order the Marines began deployment to the Iwo Jima beach.[14] Gen. Kuribayashi was far from beaten, however. In the deathly silence, landed US Marines began to slowly inch their way forward inland, oblivious to the danger. After allowing the Americans to pile up men and machinery on the beach for just over an hour, Kuribayashi unleashed the undiminished force of his countermeasures. Shortly after 10:00, everything from machine guns and mortars to heavy artillery began to rain down on the crowded beach, which was quickly transformed into a nightmarish bloodbath.[15]

At first it came as a ragged rattle of machine-gun bullets, growing gradually lower and fiercer until at last all the pent-up fury of a hundred hurricanes seemed to be breaking upon the heads of the Americans. Shells screeched and crashed, every hummock spat automatic fire and the very soft soil underfoot erupted underfoot with hundreds of exploding land mines ... Marines walking erect crumpled and fell. Concussion lifted them and slammed them down, or tore them apart ...[16]

Time-Life correspondent Robert Sherrod described it simply as "a nightmare in hell."[17]

Figure 9: *Marines wait to move inland*

The Japanese heavy artillery in Mount Suribachi opened their reinforced steel doors to fire, and then closed them immediately to prevent counterfire from the Marines and naval gunners. This made it difficult for American units to destroy a Japanese artillery piece. To make matters worse for the Americans, the bunkers were connected to the elaborate tunnel system so that bunkers that were cleared with flamethrowers and grenades were reoccupied shortly afterwards by Japanese troops moving through the tunnels. This tactic caused many casualties among the Marines, as they walked past the reoccupied bunkers without expecting to suddenly take fresh fire from them.

In response to the heavy resistance on the beach, the Army's 147th Infantry Regiment was ordered to climb from landing craft with grappling hooks to scale a high ridge about 3/4 mile from Mount Suribachi. The mission was to fire on the enemy opposing the Marine landings on the beaches below.[18] They were soon pinned down by heavy Japanese fire, and engaged in non-stop fighting for 31 days before they could be relieved.

Moving off the beaches

Amtracs, unable to do more than uselessly churn the black ash, made no progress up the slopes; their Marine passengers had to dismount and slog forward on foot.[19] Men of the Naval Construction Battalions (CBs or Seabees), braving enemy fire, eventually were able to bulldoze passages up the slopes. This allowed the Marines and equipment to finally make some progress inland and get off the jam-packed beaches. "Even so, in virtually every shell hole there lay at least one dead Marine ..."[20]

By 11:30, some Marines had managed to reach the southern tip of Airfield No. 1, whose possession had been one of the (highly unrealistic) original American objectives for the first day. The Marines endured a fanatical 100-man charge by the Japanese, but were able to keep their toehold on Airfield No. 1 as night fell. It was in this sector that Sgt. Darrell S. Cole of the 23rd Marines was killed after single-handedly knocking out several pillboxes and a bunker, thereby earning the Medal of Honor.

Crossing the island

In the left-most sector, the Americans did manage to achieve one of their objectives for the battle that day. Col. Harry B. "Harry the Horse" Liversedge the 28th Marine Regiment drove across the island at its narrowest width (approx. one-half mile), thereby isolating the Japanese dug in on Mount Suribachi.

GySgt. "Manila" John Basilone (a Medal of Honor recipient for his actions on Guadalcanal), fighting in the 27th Marines just to the right of Liversedge's 28th Regiment, was killed leading his machine-gun section. Cpl. Tony Stein, a former toolmaker, had transformed a wing gun from a wrecked fighter plane into what he called his "stinger." With this unusual weapon, he methodically killed the occupants of multiple pillboxes, allowing demolition personnel following him to destroy the position.[21] For these actions, he was (posthumously) awarded the Medal of Honor.

Action on the right flank

The right-most landing area was dominated by Japanese positions at the Quarry. The 25th Marine Regiment undertook a two-pronged attack to silence these guns. Their experience can be summarized by the ordeal of 2nd Lt. Benjamin Roselle, part of a ground team directing naval gunfire:

Within a minute a mortar shell exploded among the group ... his left foot and ankle hung from his leg, held on by a ribbon of flesh ... Within minutes a second round landed near him and fragments tore into his other leg. For nearly an hour he wondered where the next shell would land. He was soon to find out as a shell burst almost on top of him, wounding him for the third time in the shoulder. Almost at once another explosion bounced him several feet into the air and hot shards ripped into both thighs ... as he lifted his arm to look at this watch a mortar shell exploded only feet away and blasted the watch from his wrist and tore a large jagged hole in his

forearm: "I was beginning to know what it must be like to be crucified,"
he was later to say.[22]

The 25th Marines' 3rd Battalion had landed approximately 900 men in the morning. Japanese resistance at the Quarry was so fierce that by nightfall only 150 were left in fighting condition, an astounding 83.3% casualty rate.[23]

By the evening, 30,000 Marines had landed. About 40,000 more would follow. Aboard the command ship *Eldorado*, "Howlin' Mad" Smith saw the lengthy casualty reports and heard of the slow progress of the ground forces. To the war correspondents covering the operation he confessed, "I don't know who he is, but the Japanese general running this show is one smart bastard."[24]

D-Day Medals of Honor: Sgt. Darrell S. Cole, USMCR (posth.); Cpl. Tony Stein, USMCR (posth.)

Subsequent combat

In the days after the landings, the Marines expected the usual Japanese *banzai* charge during the night. This had been the standard Japanese final defense strategy in previous battles against enemy ground forces in the Pacific, such as during the Battle of Saipan. In those attacks, for which the Marines were prepared, the majority of the Japanese attackers had been killed and the Japanese strength greatly reduced. However, General Kuribayashi had strictly forbidden these "human wave" attacks by the Japanese infantrymen because he considered them to be futile.

The fighting on the beachhead at Iwo Jima was very fierce. The advance of the Marines was stalled by numerous defensive positions augmented by artillery pieces. There, the Marines were ambushed by Japanese troops who occasionally sprang out of tunnels. At night, the Japanese left their defenses under cover of darkness to attack American foxholes, but U.S. Navy ships fired star shells to deny them the cover of darkness. On Iwo Jima (and other Japanese held islands), Japanese soldiers who knew English were used to harass and or deceive Marines in order to kill them if they could; they would yell "corpsman" pretending to be a wounded Marine, in order to lure in U.S. Navy medical corpsmen attached to Marine infantry companies.

The Marines learned that firearms were relatively ineffective against the Japanese defenders and effectively used flamethrowers and grenades to flush out Japanese troops in the tunnels. One of the technological innovations of the battle, the eight Sherman M4A3R3 medium tanks equipped with a flamethrower ("Ronson" or "Zippo" tanks), proved very effective at clearing

Japanese positions. The Shermans were difficult to disable, such that defenders were often compelled to assault them in the open, where they would fall victim to the superior numbers of Marines.

Close air support was initially provided by fighters from escort carriers off the coast. This shifted over to the 15th Fighter Group, flying P-51 Mustangs, after they arrived on the island on 6 March. Similarly, illumination rounds (flares) which were used to light up the battlefield at night were initially provided by ships, shifting over later to landing force artillery. Navajo code talkers were part of the American ground communications, along with walkie-talkies and SCR-610 backpack radio sets.

After running out of water, food and most supplies, the Japanese troops became desperate toward the end of the battle. Kuribayashi, who had argued against banzai attacks at the start of the battle, realized that defeat was imminent.

Marines began to face increasing numbers of nighttime attacks; these were only repelled by a combination of machine-gun defensive positions and artillery support. At times, the Marines engaged in hand-to-hand fighting to repel the Japanese attacks. With the landing area secure, more troops and heavy equipment came ashore, and the invasion proceeded north to capture the airfields and the remainder of the island. Most Japanese soldiers fought to the death.

Raising the flag on Mt. Suribachi

"Raising the Flag on Iwo Jima" is a black and white photograph taken by Joe Rosenthal depicting six Marines from E Company, 2nd Battalion, 28th Marines, raising a U.S. flag atop Mount Suribachi on February 23, 1945, in the second of two flag-raisings on the site that day. The photograph was extremely popular, being reprinted in thousands of publications. Later, it became the only photograph to win the Pulitzer Prize for Photography in the same year as its publication, and ultimately came to be regarded as one of the most significant and recognizable images of the war, and possibly the most reproduced photograph of all time. In 1954, the flag raising picture was later used by Felix de Weldon to sculpt the Marine Corps War Memorial (Iwo Jima Memorial), located adjacent to Arlington National Cemetery.

Three of the six Marines depicted in the picture, Sergeant Michael Strank, Corporal Harlon Block, and Private First Class Franklin Sousley, were killed in action days after the flag-raising. Two of the three surviving flag-raisers, Private First Class Rene Gagnon and Private First Class Ira Hayes, together with Navy corpsman John Bradley, became celebrities upon their participation in a war bond selling tour after the battle. Two subsequent Marine Corps

Figure 10: *U.S. flag over Mount Suribachi*

Figure 11: *U.S. postage stamp, 1945 issue, commemorating the Battle of Iwo Jima*

investigations into the identities of the six men in the photograph determined in 1946 and 1947 that Henry Hansen was misidentified as being Block (both Marines died six days after the photo), and in May and June 2016 that Bradley was not in the photograph and Pfc. Harold Schultz was.[25]

By the morning of 23 February, Mount Suribachi was effectively cut off above ground from the rest of the island. The Marines knew that the Japanese defenders had an extensive network of below-ground defenses, and that in spite of its isolation above ground, the volcano was still connected to Japanese defenders via the tunnel network. They expected a fierce fight for the summit. Two small patrols from two rifle companies from 2/28 Marines were sent up the volcano to reconnoiter routes on the mountain's north face. Popular accounts (embroidered by the press in the aftermath of the release of the photo) had the Marines fighting all the way up to the summit. Although the Marine riflemen expected an ambush, one patrol encountered only small groups of Japanese defenders on top of Suribachi. The majority of the Japanese troops stayed in the tunnel network, only occasionally attacking in small groups, and were generally all killed. The recon patrols made it to the summit and scrambled down again, reporting any contact to the 2/28 Marines commander, Colonel Chandler Johnson. Johnson then called for a reinforced platoon size patrol from E Company to climb Suribachi and seize and occupy the crest. The patrol commander, 1st Lt. Harold Schrier, was handed the battalion's American flag to be raised on top to signal Suribachi's capture, if they reached the summit. Johnson and the Marines anticipated heavy fighting, but the patrol encountered only a small amount of small arms fire on the way up the mountain. Once the top was secured by Schrier and his men, a length of Japanese water pipe was found there among the wreckage, and the American flag was attached on the pipe and then raised and planted on top of Mount Suribachi which became the first foreign flag to fly on Japanese soil. Photographs of this "first flag raising" scene, taken by Marine photographer Louis R. Lowery, were not released until late 1947.

As the flag went up, Secretary of the Navy James Forrestal had just landed on the beach at the foot of Mount Suribachi and decided that he wanted the flag as a souvenir. Colonel Johnson, the battalion's commander, believed that the flag belonged to the 2nd Battalion 28th Marines, who had captured that section of the island. Johnson sent Pfc. Rene Gagnon, a messenger for E Company, to take a second larger flag up the volcano to replace the first flag. It was as the replacement flag attached to another heavy pipe went up that Rosenthal took *Raising the Flag on Iwo Jima.*

The flag flew on Mount Suribachi until it was taken down on March 14, when an American flag was officially raised at Kitano Point at the northern end of the island by orders of the commander of all the troops on Iwo Jima, Lt. Gen.

Figure 12: *Sketch of Hill 362A, made by the 31st U.S. Naval Construction Battalion. Dotted lines show the Japanese tunnel system*

Holland Smith, who witnessed the event with Maj. Gen. Graves B. Erskine, the commander of the Third Marine Division, and troops of the division.

Northern Iwo Jima

Despite Japan's loss of Mount Suribachi on the south end of the island, the Japanese still held strong positions on the north end. The rocky terrain vastly favored defense, even more so than Mount Suribachi, which was much easier to hit with naval artillery fire. Coupled with this, the fortifications constructed by Kuribayashi were more impressive than at the southern end of the island. Remaining under the command of Kuribayashi was the equivalent of eight infantry battalions, a tank regiment, and two artillery and three heavy mortar battalions. There were also about 5,000 gunners and naval infantry. The most arduous task left to the Marines was the overtaking of the Motoyama Plateau with its distinctive Hill 382 and Turkey knob and the area in between referred to as the Amphitheater. This formed the basis of what came to be known as the "meatgrinder". While this was being achieved on the right flank, the left was clearing out Hill 362 with just as much difficulty. The overall objective at this point was to take control of Airfield No. 2 in the center of the island. However, every "penetration seemed to become a disaster" as "units were raked

Figure 13: *A U.S. Marine firing his Browning M1917 machine gun at the Japanese*

from the flanks, chewed up, and sometimes wiped out. Tanks were destroyed by interlocking fire or were hoisted into the air on the spouting fireballs of buried mines". As a result, the fighting bogged down, with American casualties piling up. Even capturing these points was not a solution to the problem since a previously secured position could be attacked from the rear by the use of the tunnels and hidden pillboxes. As such, it was said that "they could take these heights at will, and then regret it".

The Marines nevertheless found ways to prevail under the circumstances. It was observed that during bombardments, the Japanese would hide their guns and themselves in the caves only to reappear when the troops would advance and lay devastating fire on them. The Japanese had over time learned basic American strategy, which was to lay heavy bombardment before an infantry attack. Consequently, General Erskine ordered the 9th Marine Regiment to attack under the cover of darkness with no preliminary barrage. This came to be a resounding success with many Japanese soldiers killed while still asleep. This was a key moment in the capture of Hill 362. It held such importance that the Japanese organized a counterattack the following night. Although Kuribayashi had forbidden the suicide charges familiar with other battles in the Pacific, the commander of the area decided on a *banzai* charge with the optimistic goal of recapturing Mount Suribachi. On the evening of 8 March, Captain Samaji

Figure 14: *March 1945 Several M4A3 Sherman tanks equipped with flamethrowers were used to clear Japanese bunkers*

Inouye and his 1,000 men charged the American lines, inflicting 347 casualties (90 deaths). The Marines counted 784 dead Japanese soldiers the next day. The same day, elements of the 3rd Marine Division reached the northern coast of the island, splitting Kuribayashi's defenses in two. There was also a *kamikaze* air attack (the only one of the battle) on the ships anchored at sea on 21 February, which resulted in the sinking of the escort carrier USS *Bismarck Sea*, severe damage to USS *Saratoga*, and slight damage to the escort carrier USS *Lunga Point*, an LST, and a transport.

Although the island was declared secure at 18:00 on 16 March (25 days after the landings), the 5th Marine Division still faced Kuribayashi's stronghold in a gorge 640 m (700 yd) long at the northwestern end of the island. On 21 March, the Marines destroyed the command post in the gorge with four tons of explosives and on 24 March, Marines sealed the remaining caves at the northern tip of the island. However, on the night of 25 March, a 300-man Japanese force launched a final counterattack in the vicinity of Airfield No. 2. Army pilots, Seabees, and Marines of the 5th Pioneer Battalion and 28th Marines fought the Japanese force for up to 90 minutes, suffering heavy casualties (53 killed, 120 wounded).Wikipedia:Citation needed Two Marines from the 36th Depot Company, an all-African-American unit, received the Bronze Star. First Lieutenant Harry Martin of the 5th Pioneer Battalion was the last

Marine to be awarded the Medal of Honor during the battle. Although still a matter of speculation because of conflicting accounts from surviving Japanese veterans, it has been said that Kuribayashi led this final assault, which unlike the loud *banzai* charge of previous battles, was characterized as a silent attack. If ever proven true, Kuribayashi would have been the highest ranking Japanese officer to have personally led an attack during World War II. Additionally, this would also be Kuribayashi's final act, a departure from the normal practice of the commanding Japanese officers committing seppuku behind the lines while the rest perished in the *banzai* charge, as happened during the battles of Saipan and Okinawa. The island was officially declared secure at 09:00 on 26 March.

Once the island was officially declared secure, the Army's 147th Infantry Regiment was ostensibly there to act as a garrison force, but they soon found themselves locked in a bitter struggle against thousands of stalwart defenders engaging in a last-ditch guerilla campaign to harass the Americans.[26] Using well-supplied caves and tunnel systems, the Japanese resisted American advances. For three months, the 147th slogged across the island, using flamethrowers, grenades, and satchel charges to dig out the enemy, killing some 1,602 Japanese soldiers in small unit actions.

Weapons

The United States M2 flamethrower was heavily used in the Pacific. It features two tanks containing fuel and compressed gas respectively, which are combined and ignited to produce a stream of flaming liquid out of the tip. These flamethrowers were used to kill Japanese holed into pillboxes, buildings and caves. A battalion would assign one flamethrower per platoon with one reserve flamethrower in each group. Flamethrower operators were usually in more danger than regular troops as the short range of their weapon required close combat, and the visibility of the flames on the battlefield made them a prominent target for snipers. Still they were essential to breaking the enemy and one battalion commander called the flamethrower the "best single weapon of the operation."

Marines later experimented putting flamethrowers on tanks which were also deployed during battle. Their effectiveness was more limited due to Iwo Jima's rough terrain. A flamethrower tank would have a range of approximately 100 yd (90 m), carry 300 gallons of fuel and have a firing time of 150 seconds.

Figure 15: *A flamethrower operator of E Company, 2nd Battalion 9th Marines, 3rd Marine Division, runs under fire on Iwo Jima*

Aftermath

The last of these holdouts on the island, two of Lieutenant Toshihiko Ohno's men, Yamakage Kufuku and Matsudo Linsoki, lasted four years without being caught and finally surrendered on 6 January 1949.

Though ultimately victorious, the American victory at Iwo Jima had come at a terrible price. According to the official Navy Department Library website, "The 36-day (Iwo Jima) assault resulted in more than 26,000 American casualties, including 6,800 dead." By comparison, the much larger scale 82-day Battle of Okinawa lasting from early April until mid-June 1945 (involving five U.S. Army and two Marine Corps divisions) resulted in of over 62,000 U.S. casualties, of whom over 12,000 were killed or missing. Iwo Jima was also the only U.S. Marine battle where the American casualties exceeded the Japanese, although Japanese combat deaths numbered three times as many as American deaths. Two US Marines were captured during the battle, neither of whom survived their captivity. USS *Bismarck Sea* was also lost, the last U.S. aircraft carrier sunk in World War II. Because all civilians had been evacuated, there were no civilian casualties at Iwo Jima, unlike at Saipan and Okinawa.

Figure 16: *U.S. Marines pose on top of enemy pillbox with a captured Japanese flag*

Strategic importance

In hindsight, given the number of casualties, the necessity and long-term significance of the island's capture to the outcome of the war became a contentious issue and remains disputed. The Marines, who suffered the actual casualties, were not consulted in the planning of the operation.[27] As early as April 1945, retired Chief of Naval Operations William V. Pratt stated in *Newsweek* magazine that considering the "expenditure of manpower to acquire a small, God-forsaken island, useless to the Army as a staging base and useless to the Navy as a fleet base ... [one] wonders if the same sort of airbase could not have been reached by acquiring other strategic localities at lower cost."

The lessons learned on Iwo Jima served as guidelines for the following Battle of Okinawa and the planned invasion of the Japanese homeland. For example, "because of the casualties taken at Iwo Jima on the first day, it was decided to make the preparatory bombardment the heaviest yet delivered on to a Pacific island".[28] Also, in the planning for a potential attack on the Japanese home islands, it was taken into account that around a third of the troops committed to Iwo Jima and again at Okinawa had been killed or wounded.[29]

The justification for Iwo Jima's strategic importance to the United States' war effort has been that it provided a landing and refueling site for long-range fighter

Figure 17: *Lieutenant Wade discusses the overall importance of the target at a pre-invasion briefing.*

Figure 18: *American supplies being landed at Iwo Jima.*

Figure 19: *Marines from the 24th Marine Regiment during the Battle of Iwo Jima*

escorts. These escorts proved both impractical and unnecessary, and only ten such missions were ever flown from Iwo Jima.

Japanese fighter aircraft based on Iwo Jima sometimes attacked AAF planes, which were vulnerable on their way to Japan because they were heavily laden with bombs and fuel. However, although some Japanese interceptors were based on Iwo Jima, their impact on the American bombing effort was marginal; in the three months before the invasion only 11 B-29s were lost as a result. The Superfortresses found it unnecessary to make any major detour around the island.[30]

The Japanese on Iwo Jima had radar and were thus able to notify their comrades at home of incoming B-29 Superfortresses flying from the Mariana Islands. However, the capture of Iwo Jima did not affect the Japanese early-warning radar system, which continued to receive information on incoming B-29s from the island of Rota (which was never invaded).[31]

As early as 4 March 1945, while fighting was still taking place, the B-29 *Dinah Might* of the USAAF 9th Bomb Group reported it was low on fuel near the island and requested an emergency landing. Despite enemy fire, the airplane landed on the Allied-controlled section of the island (South Field), without incident, and was serviced, refueled and departed.

In all, 2,251 B-29 landings on Iwo Jima were recorded during the war. Muskin records that 1,191 fighter escorts and 3,081 strike sorties were flown from Iwo Jima against Japan.

Some downed B-29 crewmen were saved by air-sea rescue aircraft and vessels operating from the island, but Iwo Jima was only one of many islands that could have been used for such a purpose. As for the importance of the island as a landing and refueling site for bombers, Marine Captain Robert Burrell, then a history instructor at the United States Naval Academy, suggested that only a small proportion of the 2,251 landings were for genuine emergencies, the great majority possibly being for minor technical checkups, training, or refueling. According to Burrell,

> *This justification became prominent only after the Marines seized the island and incurred high casualties. The tragic cost of Operation Detachment pressured veterans, journalists, and commanders to fixate on the most visible rationalization for the battle. The sight of the enormous, costly, and technologically sophisticated B-29 landing on the island's small airfield most clearly linked Iwo Jima to the strategic bombing campaign. As the myths about the flag raisings on Mount Suribachi reached legendary proportions, so did the emergency landing theory in order to justify the need to raise that flag.*

In publishing *The Ghosts of Iwo Jima*, Texas A&M University Press said that the very losses formed the basis for a "reverence for the Marine Corps" that not only embodied the "American national spirit" but ensured the "institutional survival" of the Marine Corps.

Medal of Honor recipients

The Medal of Honor is the highest military decoration awarded by the United States government. It is bestowed on a member of the United States armed forces who distinguishes himself by "... conspicuous gallantry and intrepidity at the risk of his life above and beyond the call of duty while engaged in an action against an enemy of the United States ..." Because of its nature, the medal is commonly awarded posthumously; since its creation during the American Civil War it has been presented only 3,464 times.

The Medal of Honor was awarded to 27 U.S. Marines and U.S. sailors (14 posthumously), during the battle of Iwo Jima. 22 medals were presented to Marines (12 posthumously) and 5 were presented to sailors, 4 of whom were hospital corpsmen (2 posthumously) attached to Marine infantry units; 22 Medals of Honor was 28% of the 82 awarded to Marines in World War II.

Figure 20: *Harry Truman congratulates Marine Corporal Hershel Williams of the Third Marine Division on being awarded the Medal of Honor, 5 October 1945*

Hershel W. Williams (Marine Corps) is the only living Medal of Honor recipient from the Battle of Iwo Jima. Williams (age 94 in 2018) is one of four living Medal of Honor recipients of World War II; three soldiers and one Marine.

Legacy

The Marine Corps War Memorial (Iwo Jima Memorial) was dedicated on 10 November 1954.

The United States Navy has commissioned two ships with the name USS *Iwo Jima* (LPH-2) (1961–1993) and USS *Iwo Jima* (LHD-7) (2001–present).

On 19 February 1985, the 40th anniversary of the landings on Iwo Jima, an event called the "Reunion of Honor" was held (the event has been held annually since 2002). The veterans of both sides who fought in the battle of Iwo Jima attended the event. The place was the invasion beach where U.S. forces landed. A memorial on which inscriptions were engraved by both sides was built at the center of the meeting place. Japanese attended at the mountain side, where the Japanese inscription was carved, and Americans attended at the shore side, where the English inscription was carved.[32] After unveiling and offering of flowers were made, the representatives of both countries approached the memorial; upon meeting, they shook hands. The combined Japan-U.S. memorial service of the 50th anniversary of the battle was held in front of the monument in February 1995.[33] Further memorial services have been held on later anniversaries.Wikipedia:Citation needed

The importance of the battle to Marines today is demonstrated in pilgrimages made to the island, and specifically the summit of Suribachi. Marines will often leave dog tags, rank insignia, or other tokens at the monuments in homage.[34] Iwo Jima Day is observed annually on 19 February in the Commonwealth of Massachusetts with a ceremony at the State House.

The Japanese government continues to search for and retrieve the remains of Japanese military personnel who were killed during the battle.[35]

Figure 21: *The U.S. Marine Corps War Memorial in Arlington, Virginia*

Figure 22: *The memorial on top of Suribachi*

Figure 23: *The 60th anniversary reunion at the Japanese part of the memorial*

Movies and documentaries

- *To the Shores of Iwo Jima*, a 1945 American documentary produced by the United States Navy, Marine Corps, and the Coast Guard.
- *Glamour Gal*, a 1945 film about Marine artillery.
- *Sands of Iwo Jima*, a 1949 American film starring John Wayne.
- *The Outsider*, a 1961 film starring Tony Curtis as the conflicted flag raiser Ira Hayes.
- Episode 23 from the acclaimed 1973 Thames Television documentary *The World at War*.
- *The League of Grateful Sons*, a 2005 documentary by Vision Forum.
- *Flags of Our Fathers* and *Letters from Iwo Jima*, two 2006 films directed by Clint Eastwood. *Flags of Our Fathers* is filmed from the American perspective and is based on the book by James Bradley and Ron Powers (*Flags of Our Fathers*). *Letters from Iwo Jima* (originally titled *Red Sun, Black Sand*) is filmed from the Japanese perspective.
- *Battle Rats: Iwo Jima* (2009) (TV).
- Part 8 of the 2010 HBO miniseries *The Pacific*, produced by Tom Hanks and Steven Spielberg, includes part of the Battle of Iwo Jima from the point of view of John Basilone from the beginning of the invasion until his death later in the day.

References

<templatestyles src="Template:Refbegin/styles.css" />

- Allen, Robert E. (2004). *The First Battalion of the 28th Marines on Iwo Jima: A Day-by-Day History from Personal Accounts and Official Reports, with Complete Muster Rolls.* Jefferson, N.C.: McFarland & Company. ISBN 0-7864-0560-0. OCLC 41157682[36].
- Bradley, James; Ron Powers (2001) [2000]. *Flags of Our Fathers.* New York: Bantam. ISBN 0-553-38029-X. OCLC 48215748[37].
- Bradley, James (2003). *Flyboys: A True Story of Courage.* Boston: Little, Brown and Company. ISBN 0-316-10584-8. OCLC 52071383[38].
- Buell, Hal (2006). *Uncommon Valor, Common Virtue: Iwo Jima and the Photograph that Captured America.* New York: Penguin Group. ISBN 0-425-20980-6. OCLC 65978720[39].
- Burrell, Robert S. "Breaking the Cycle of Iwo Jima Mythology: A Strategic Study of Operation Detachment," *Journal of Military History* Volume 68, Number 4, October 2004, pp. 1143–1186 and rebuttal in Project MUSE[40]
- Burrell, Robert S. (2006). *The Ghosts of Iwo Jima.* College Station: Texas A&M University Press. ISBN 1-58544-483-9. OCLC 61499920[41].
- Eldridge, Robert D.; Charles W. Tatum (2011). *Fighting Spirit: The Memoirs of Major Yoshitaka Horie and the Battle of Iwo Jima.* Annapolis: Naval Institute Press. ISBN 978-1-59114-856-2.
- Hammel, Eric (2006). *Iwo Jima: Portrait of a Battle: United States Marines at War in the Pacific.* St. Paul, Minn.: Zenith Press. ISBN 0-7603-2520-0. OCLC 69104268[42].
- Hearn, Chester (2003). *Sorties into @#!* % : The Hidden War on Chichi Jima.* Westport, Conn.: Praeger Publishers. ISBN 0-275-98081-2. OCLC 51968985[43].
- Kakehashi, Kumiko (2007). *So Sad to Fall in Battle: An Account of War Based on General Tadamichi Kuribayashi's Letters from Iwo Jima.* Presidio Press. ISBN 0-89141-917-9.
- Kirby, Lawrence F. (1995). *Stories From The Pacific: The Island War 1942–1945.* Manchester, Mass.: The Masconomo Press. ISBN 0-9645103-1-6. OCLC 32971472[44].
- Leckie, Robert (2005) [1967]. *The Battle for Iwo Jima.* New York: ibooks, Inc. ISBN 1-59019-241-9. OCLC 56015751[45].
- Linenthal, Edward T. "Shaping a Heroic Presence: Iwo Jima in American Memory". *Reviews in American History* Vol. 21, No. 1 (March 1993), pp. 8–12. JSTOR 2702942[46].

- Lucas, Jack; D. K. Drum (2006). *Indestructible: The Unforgettable Story of a Marine Hero at the Battle of Iwo Jima*. Cambridge, Mass.: Da Capo Press. ISBN 0-306-81470-6. OCLC 68175700[47].
- Morison, Samuel Eliot (2002) [1970]. *Victory in the Pacific, 1945*, vol. 14 of *History of United States Naval Operations in World War II*. Urbana, Ill.: University of Illinois Press. ISBN 0-252-07065-8. OCLC 49784806[48].
- Newcomb, Richard F.; Harry Schmidt (2002) [1965]. *Iwo Jima*. New York: Owl Books. ISBN 0-8050-7071-0. OCLC 48951047[49].
- Overton, Richard E. (2006). *God Isn't Here: A Young American's Entry into World War II and His Participation in the Battle for Iwo Jima*. Clearfield, Utah: American Legacy Media. ISBN 0-9761547-0-6. OCLC 60694955[50].
- Rawson, Andrew. 2016. *Iwo Jima 1945*, Toronto: Dundurn.
- Ross, Bill D. (1986) [1985]. *Iwo Jima: Legacy of Valor*. New York: Vintage. ISBN 0-394-74288-5. OCLC 13582622[51].
- Shively, John C. (2006). *The Last Lieutenant: A Foxhole View of the Epic Battle for Iwo Jima*. Bloomington: Indiana University Press. ISBN 0-253-34728-9. OCLC 61761637[52].
- Toyn, Gary W. (2006). *The Quiet Hero: The Untold Medal of Honor Story of George E. Wahlen at the Battle for Iwo Jima*. Clearfield, Utah: American Legacy Media. ISBN 0-9761547-1-4. OCLC 72161745[53].
- Veronee, Marvin D. (2001). *A portfolio of photographs: selected to illustrate the setting for my experience in the battle of Iwo Jima, World War II, Pacific theater*. Quantico: Visionary Pub. ISBN 0-9715928-2-9. OCLC 52001277[54].
- Wells, John K. (1995). *Give Me Fifty Marines Not Afraid to Die: Iwo Jima*. Abilene, Tex.: Quality Publications. ISBN 0-9644675-0-X. OCLC 32153036[55].
- Wheeler, Richard (1994) [1980]. *Iwo*. Annapolis, Md.: Naval Institute Press. ISBN 1-55750-922-0. OCLC 31693687[56].
- Wheeler, Richard (1994) [1965]. *The @#!* % Battle for Suribachi*. Annapolis, Md.: Naval Institute Press. ISBN 1-55750-923-9. OCLC 31970164[57].
- Wright, Derrick (2007) [1999]. *The Battle for Iwo Jima 1945*. Stroud: Sutton Publishing. ISBN 0-7509-4544-3. OCLC 67871973[58].
- Wright, Derrick (2004) [2001]. *Iwo Jima 1945: The Marines Raise the Flag On Mount Suribachi*. Oxford: Osprey Publishing Ltd. ISBN 0-275-98273-4.
- Kindersley, Dorling (2009). *World War II: The Definitive Visual History*. DK Publishing.

Online

<templatestyles src="Template:Refbegin/styles.css" />

- Alexander, Joseph H. (1994). *Closing In: Marines in the Seizure of Iwo Jima*[59]. Marines in World War II Commemorative Series. Washington, D.C.: History and Museums Division, Headquarters, United States Marine Corps. OCLC 32194668[60].
- Bartley, Whitman S. (1954). *Iwo Jima: Amphibious Epic*[61]. Marines in World War II Historical Monograph. Washington, D.C.: Historical, Division of Public Information, Headquarters, United States Marine Corps. OCLC 28592680[62].
- Garand, George W.; Truman R. Strobridge (1971). "Part VI: Iwo Jima". *Western Pacific Operations*[63]. Volume IV of History of U.S. Marine Corps Operations in World War II. Historical Branch, United States Marine Corps. ISBN 0-89839-198-9.
- Dyer, George Carroll (1956). "The Amphibians Came to Conquer: The Story of Admiral Richmond Kelly Turner"[64]. United States Government Printing Office. Archived[65] from the original on 21 May 2011. Retrieved 5 May 2011.
- "Animated Map History of The Battle of Iwo Jima (including Medal of Honor citations)"[66]. HistoryAnimated.com.
- "The Battle for Iwo Jima (color combat footage)"[67]. SonicBomb.com.
- Brady, John H. "Iwo Jima"[68]. Iwo Jima, Inc.
- "Battle of Iwo Jima"[69]. WW2DB.com. Site contains 250 photographs.
- Williams, Greg. "Dimensions of Valor"[70]. *Tampa Tribune*. TBO.com. Archived from the original[71] (Flash) on 5 December 2006. 3-D stereo photograph of Iwo Jima flag-raising.
- "Mt. Suribachi HDR Image"[72]. *Japan Photos*. February 2007.Wikipedia:Link rot A tone-mapped High Dynamic Range Image of Iwo Jima.
- "Iwo Jima: Forgotten Valor"[73]. *Primary Source Adventures*. Portal to Texas History, University of North Texas.
- Dawson, Rick (2007). "The Battle of Iwo Jima"[74]. ArticleMyriad.com. Archived from the original[75] on 26 February 2007.
- "Iwo Jima Combat Footage in Color"[76]. WW2incolor.com.
- Lemer, Jeremy (15 February 2005). "Remembering the Battle of Iwo Jima"[77]. Columbia News Service. Archived from the original[78] on 8 September 2006. Retrieved 6 October 2006.
- "Operations map of Iwo Jima"[79] (JPG). 23 October 1944.
- "Collection of military maps of Iwo Jima"[80]. Historical Resources. 15 September 2008. Archived from the original[81] on 8 January 2009. Retrieved 16 July 2017.

- "To the Shores of Iwo Jima"[82] (video). Google Video.
- "Battle of Iwo Jima"[83]. History of War.
- Alexander, Colonel Joseph (2000). "Battle of Iwo Jima"[84]. HistoryNet.com and World War II magazine.
- "Iwo Jima Pictures"[85]. WW2-Pictures.com. Archived from the original[86] on 16 April 2010.
- "Amphibious Operations: Capture of Iwo Jima"[87]. Naval History and Heritage Command. Retrieved 5 September 2015.
- "Victory At Sea: Target Suribachi"[88] (video). Internet Archive. Archived[89] from the original on 12 February 2009. Retrieved 17 January 2009.
- "Rare photos of the Battle of Iwo Jima from the U.S. National Archives and the Department of Defense, USMC"[90]. Awesome Stories. Retrieved 9 March 2010.
- "Daily summaries of fighting, Medal of Honor citations, a listing of those who died on Iwo Jima, and maps of the battle"[91]. Iwojimahistory.com. Retrieved 8 November 2011.

External links

- 🌐 Media related to Battle of Iwo Jima at Wikimedia Commons

Coordinates: 24°47′N 141°19′E[92]

Planning and preparation

Planning for the Battle of Iwo Jima

In **anticipation of the Battle of Iwo Jima**, Lieutenant General Tadamichi Kuribayashi prepared a defense that broke with Japanese military doctrine. Rather than defending the beaches, Kuribayashi devised a defense that maximized enemy attrition. The American plan of attack was made in anticipation of a standard defense.

Japanese planning

Even before the fall of Saipan in June 1944, Japanese planners knew that Iwo Jima would have to be reinforced significantly if it were to be held for any length of time, and preparations were made to send sizable numbers of men and quantities of materiel to that island. In late May, Lieutenant General Tadamichi Kuribayashi was summoned to the office of the Prime Minister, General Hideki Tōjō, and told that he had been chosen to defend Iwo Jima to the last. Kuribayashi was further apprised of the importance of this assignment when Tojo pointed out that the eyes of the entire nation were focused on the defense of Iwo Jima. Fully aware of the implications of the task, the general accepted, and by 8 June 1944, Kuribayashi was on his way to convert Iwo Jima into an impregnable fortress.

When he arrived, some 80 fighter aircraft were stationed on Iwo Jima, but by early July only four remained. A United States Navy force then came within sight of the island and bombarded it for two days, destroying every building and the four remaining aircraft.

Much to the surprise of the Japanese garrison on Iwo Jima, there was no American attempt to invade the island during the summer of 1944. There was little doubt that in time the Americans would attack, and General Kuribayashi was more determined than ever to exact the heaviest possible price for Iwo Jima,

Figure 24: *View of the invasion beach from
the top of Mount Suribachi, February 2002*

although the lack of naval and air support meant that Iwo Jima could not hold
out indefinitely against an invader with sea and air supremacy.

By late July, Kuribayashi had evacuated all civilians from the island. Lieutenant
General Hideyoshi Obata, commanding general of the 31st Army, early in
1944 had been responsible for the defense of Iwo Jima prior to his return to
the Marianas. Following the doctrine that an invasion had to be met practically
at the water's edge, Obata had ordered the emplacement of artillery and the
construction of pillboxes near the beaches. General Kuribayashi had a different
strategy. Instead of attempting to hold the beaches, he planned to defend them
with a sprinkling of automatic weapons and infantry. Artillery, mortars, and
rockets would be emplaced on the foot and slopes of Mount Suribachi, as well
as in the high ground to the north of Chidori airfield.

The reason for Kuribayashi's departure from the water's edge defense strategy,
which had been the normal practice for the Japanese Imperial Army, was that
he predicted that American air and naval bombardments would destroy any
defenses on the beaches. It had been used at Saipan to great losses for the
Japanese. For water's edge defense to work, it needed support from the air
and sea, none of which the Japanese Imperial Navy was capable of mounting
at this point anymore. However, other military branches, especially the navy,

Figure 25: *Sketch of Hill 362A, made by the 31st U.S. Naval Construction Battalion. Dotted lines show the underground Japanese tunnel system*

were still insistent on the water's edge defense and demanded that Kuribayashi see to it. In the end Kuribayashi had some pillboxes built at the beach as a token measure. The pillboxes were destroyed by American bombardment.

Caves, bunkers and tunnels

A prolonged defense of the island required the preparation of an extensive system of caves and tunnels, for the naval bombardment had clearly shown that surface installations could not withstand extensive shelling. To this end, mining engineers were dispatched from Japan to draw blueprints for projected underground fortifications that would consist of elaborate tunnels at varying levels to assure good ventilation and minimize the effect of bombs or shells exploding near the entrances or exits.

At the same time, reinforcements were gradually beginning to reach the island. As commander of the 109th Infantry Division, General Kuribayashi decided first of all to shift the 2nd Independent Mixed Brigade, consisting of about 5,000 men under Major General Kotau Osuga, from Chichi to Iwo Jima. With the fall of Saipan, 2,700 men of the 145th Infantry Regiment, commanded by Colonel Masuo Ikeda, were diverted to Iwo Jima. These reinforcements, who reached the island during July and August 1944, brought the strength of the garrison up to approximately 12,700 men. Next came 1,233 men of the 204th Naval Construction Battalion, who quickly set to work constructing concrete pillboxes and other fortifications.

On 10 August 1944, Rear Admiral Rinosuke Ichimaru reached Iwo Jima, shortly followed by 2,216 naval personnel, including naval aviators and ground crews. The admiral, a renowned Japanese aviator, had been crippled in an airplane crash in the mid-twenties and, ever since the outbreak of the war, had chafed under repeated rear echelon assignments.

For the remainder of 1944, the construction of fortifications on Iwo also went into high gear. The Japanese were quick to discover that the black volcanic ash that existed in abundance all over the island could be converted into concrete of superior quality when mixed with cement. Pillboxes near the beaches north of Mount Suribachi were constructed of reinforced concrete, many of them with walls four feet thick. At the same time, an elaborate system of caves, concrete blockhouses, and pillboxes were established. One of the results of American air attacks and naval bombardment in the early summer of 1944 had been to drive the Japanese so deep underground that eventually their defenses became virtually immune to air or naval bombardment.

While the Japanese on Peleliu Island in the Western Carolines, also awaiting American invasion, had turned the improvement of natural caves into an art, the defenders of Iwo developed it into a science. Because of the importance of the underground positions, 25% of the garrison was detailed to tunneling. Positions constructed underground ranged in size from small caves for a few men to several underground chambers capable of holding 300 or 400 men. In order to prevent personnel from becoming trapped in any one excavation, the subterranean installations were provided with multiple entrances and exits, as well as stairways and interconnecting passageways. Special attention had to be paid to providing adequate ventilation, since sulphur fumes were present in many of the underground installations. Fortunately for the Japanese, most of the volcanic stone on Iwo was so soft that it could be cut with hand tools.

General Kuribayashi established his command post in the northern part of the island, about 500 m northeast of Kita village and south of Kitano Point. This installation, 20 m underground, consisted of caves of varying sizes, connected by 150 m of tunnels. Here the island commander had his own war room in one of three small concrete enclosed chambers; the two similar rooms were used by the staff. Farther south on Hill 382, the second highest elevation on the island, the Japanese constructed a radio and weather station. Nearby, on an elevation just southeast of the station, an enormously large blockhouse was constructed which served as the headquarters of Colonel Chosaku Kaidō, who commanded all artillery on Iwo Jima. Other hills in the northern portion of the island were tunnelled out. All of these major excavations featured multiple entrances and exits and were virtually invulnerable to damage from artillery or aerial bombardment. Typical of the thoroughness employed in the construction of subterranean defenses was the main communications center south of Kita village, which was so spacious that it contained a chamber 50 m long and 20 m wide. This giant structure was similar in construction and thickness of walls and ceilings to General Kuribayashi's command post. A 150 m tunnel 20 m below the ground led into this vast subterranean chamber.

Perhaps the most ambitious construction project to get under way was the creation of an underground passageway designed to link all major defense installations on the island. As projected, this passageway was to have attained a total length of almost 27 km (17 mi). Had it been completed, it would have linked the formidable underground installations in the northern portion of Iwo Jima with the southern part of the island, where the northern slope of Mount Suribachi alone harbored several thousand yards of tunnels. By the time the Marines landed on Iwo Jima, more than 18 km (11 mi) of tunnels had been completed.Wikipedia:Citation needed

A supreme effort was required of the Japanese personnel engaged in the underground construction work. Aside from the heavy physical labor, the men were exposed to heat from 30–50 °C (86–122 °F), as well as sulphur fumes that forced them to wear gas masks. In numerous instances a work detail had to be relieved after only five minutes. Renewed American air attacks struck the island on 8 December 1944 and became a daily occurrence until the actual invasion of the island. Subsequently, a large number of men had to be diverted to repairing the damaged airfields.

Artillery

Next to arrive on Iwo Jima were artillery units and five anti-tank battalions. Even though numerous supply ships en route to Iwo Jima were sunk by American submarines and aircraft, substantial quantities of materiel did reach Iwo Jima during the summer and autumn of 1944. By the end of the year, General Kuribayashi had available to him 361 artillery pieces of 75 mm or larger caliber, a dozen 320 mm mortars, 65 medium (150 mm) and light (81 mm) mortars, 33 naval guns 80 mm or larger, and 94 anti-aircraft guns 75 mm or larger. In addition to this formidable array of large caliber guns, the Iwo Jima defenses could boast more than 200 20 mm and 25 mm anti-aircraft guns and 69 37 mm and 47 mm antitank guns.

The firepower of the artillery was further augmented with a variety of rockets varying from an eight-inch type that weighed 90 kg and could travel 2–3 km, to a giant 250 kg projectile that had a range of more than 7 km. Altogether, 70 rocket guns and their crews reached Iwo Jima.

Figure 26: *Japanese 120 mm gun after the battle on Iwo Jima (knocked-out prior to D-Day)*

Tanks

In order to further strengthen the Iwo defenses, the 26th Tank Regiment, which had been stationed at Pusan, Korea after extended service in Manchuria, received orders to head for Iwo Jima. The officer commanding this regiment was Lieutenant Colonel Baron Takeichi Nishi, a 1932 Olympic gold medallist. The regiment, consisting of 600 men and 28 tanks, sailed from Japan in mid-July on board the *Nisshu Maru*. On 18 July 1944, as the ship, sailing in a convoy, approached Chichi Jima, it was torpedoed by an American submarine, USS *Cobia*. Even though only two members of the 26th Tank Regiment were killed, all of the regiment's 28 tanks went to the bottom of the sea. It would be December before these tanks could be replaced. The 22 tanks which finally reached Iwo Jima included medium Type 97 Chi-Ha and light Type 95 Ha-Go tanks. Neither of these types were near comparable to the better armed and better armored M4 Sherman medium tanks fielded by the Americans.

Initially, Colonel Nishi had planned to employ his armor as a type of "roving fire brigade", to be committed at focal points of combat. The rugged terrain precluded such employment and, in the end, the tanks were deployed in static positions under the colonel's watchful eyes. They were either buried or their turrets were dismounted and so skillfully emplaced in the rocky ground that they were practically invisible from the air or the ground. The headquarters of the 26th Tank Regiment, which was located near the village of Maruman, was moved to the eastern part of the island when the battle began.

Defense planning

While Iwo Jima was being converted into a major fortress with all possible speed, General Kuribayashi formulated his final plans for the defense of the island. This plan, which constituted a radical departure from the defensive tactics used by the Japanese earlier in the war, provided for the following major points:

1. In order to prevent disclosing their positions to the Americans, Japanese artillery was to remain silent during the expected prelanding bombardment. No fire would be directed against the American naval vessels.
2. Upon landing on Iwo Jima, the Americans were not to encounter any opposition on the beaches.
3. Once the Americans had advanced about 500 m inland, they were to be taken under the concentrated fire of automatic weapons stationed in the vicinity of Motoyama airfield to the north, as well as automatic weapons and artillery emplaced both on the high ground to the north of the landing beaches and Mount Suribachi to the south.
4. After inflicting maximum possible casualties and damage on the landing force, the artillery was to displace northward from the high ground near the Chidori airfield.

In this connection, Kuribayashi stressed once again that he planned to conduct an elastic defense designed to wear down the invasion force. Such prolonged resistance naturally required the defending force to stockpile rations and ammunition. To this end the island commander accumulated a food reserve to last for two and a half months, ever mindful of the fact that the trickle of supplies that was reaching Iwo Jima during the latter part of 1944 would cease altogether once the island was surrounded by a hostile naval force.

During the final months of preparing Iwo Jima for the defense, General Kuribayashi saw to it that the strenuous work of building fortifications did not interfere with the training of units. As an initial step towards obtaining more time for training, he ordered work on the northernmost airfield on the island halted. In an operations order issued in early December, the island commander set 11 February 1945 as the target date for completion of defensive preparations and specified that personnel were to spend 70% of their time in training and 30% in construction work.

Despite intermittent harassment by American submarines and aircraft, additional personnel continued to arrive on Iwo until February 1945. By that time

General Kuribayashi had under his command a force totaling between 21,000 and 23,000 men, including both Army and Navy units.

Lines of defense

General Kuribayashi made several changes in his basic defense plan in the months preceding the American invasion of Iwo Jima. The final strategy, which became effective in January 1945, called for the creation of strong, mutually supporting positions which were to be defended to the death. Neither large scale counterattacks, withdrawals, nor banzai charges were contemplated. The southern portion of Iwo in the proximity of Mount Suribachi was organized into a semi-independent defense sector. Fortifications included casemated coast artillery and automatic weapons in mutually supporting pillboxes. The narrow isthmus to the north of Suribachi was to be defended by a small infantry force. On the other hand, this entire area was exposed to the fire of artillery, rocket launchers, and mortars emplaced on Suribachi to the south and the high ground to the north.

A main line of defense, consisting of mutually supporting positions in depth, extended from the northwestern part of the island to the southeast, along a general line from the cliffs to the northwest, across Motoyama Airfield No. 2 to Minami village. From there it continued eastward to the shoreline just south of Tachiiwa Point. The entire line of defense was dotted with pillboxes, bunkers, and blockhouses. Colonel Nishi's immobilized tanks, carefully dug in and camouflaged, further reinforced this fortified area, whose strength was supplemented by the broken terrain. A second line of defense extended from a few hundred yards south of Kitano Point at the very northern tip of Iwo across the still uncompleted Airfield No. 3, to Motoyama village, and then to the area between Tachiiwa Point and the East Boat Basin. This second line contained fewer man-made fortifications, but the Japanese took maximum advantage of natural caves and other terrain features.

As an additional means of protecting the two completed airfields on Iwo from direct assault, the Japanese constructed a number of antitank ditches near the fields and mined all natural routes of approach. When, on 2 January, more than a dozen B-24 Liberator bombers raided Airfield No. 1 and inflicted heavy damage, Kuribayashi diverted more than 600 men, 11 trucks, and 2 bulldozers for immediate repairs, rendering the airfield operational within only 12 hours. Eventually, 2,000 men were assigned the job of filling the bomb craters, with as many as 50 men detailed to one crater. By the end of 1944 American B-24 bombers were over Iwo Jima almost every night, and U.S. Navy carriers and cruisers frequently sortied into the Ogasawaras. On 8 December 1944, American aircraft dropped more than 800 tons of bombs on Iwo Jima, which did very little real damage to the island defenses. Even though frequent air raids

Figure 27: *Holland Smith, commander of the assaulting U.S. forces*

interfered with the Japanese defensive preparations and robbed the garrison of badly needed sleep, work was not materially slowed.

As early as 5 January 1945, Admiral Ichimaru conducted a briefing of naval personnel at his command post in which he informed them of the destruction of the Japanese Fleet at the Battle of Leyte Gulf, the loss of the Philippines, and the expectation that Iwo would shortly be invaded. Exactly one month later, Japanese radio operators on Iwo reported to the island commander that code signals of American aircraft had undergone an ominous change. On 13 February, a Japanese naval patrol plane spotted 170 American ships moving north-westward from Saipan. All Japanese troops in the Ogasawaras were alerted and occupied their battle positions. On Iwo Jima, preparations for the pending battle had been completed, and the defenders were ready.

American planning

The origins of the battle lie in the complex politics of the Pacific theater, in which operational control was divided between the South West Pacific Area (command) of General Douglas MacArthur and the Pacific Ocean Areas (command) led by Admiral Chester Nimitz. The potential for interservice rivalry between the Army and Navy created by this partition of responsibility was exacerbated by similar divisions within the Joint Chiefs of Staff (JCS) in Washington. By September 1944, the two services could not come to an agreement about the main direction of advance towards the Japanese home islands in the coming year. The Army was pressing for the chief effort to be an invasion of Formosa (Taiwan), in which MacArthur would be in overall command and in which it would predominate.

The Navy however preferred the idea of an operation against Okinawa, which would be a mainly seaborne effort. Seeking to gain leverage and so break the impasse, on 29 September Nimitz suggested to Admiral Ernest King that as a preliminary to the Okinawa offensive the island of Iwo Jima could be taken. The tiny island lacked harbors and so was of no direct interest to the Navy, but for some time General Henry Harley Arnold of the U.S. Army Air Forces had been lobbying to take Iwo Jima. He argued that an airbase there would provide useful fighter escort cover for the B-29 Superfortresses of his XX Bomber Command, then beginning its strategic bombing campaign against the Japanese home islands (the later role of Iwo Jima as a refueling station for B-29s played no part in the original decision-making process). Arnold's support in the JCS enabled the Navy to get Okinawa rather than Formosa approved as the main target on 2 October.[93] At this time the Iwo Jima invasion was expected to be a brief prologue to the main campaign, with relatively light casualties; King assumed that Nimitz would be able to reuse three of the Marine Corps divisions assigned to Iwo Jima for the attack on Okinawa, which was originally scheduled to take place just forty days later.

On 7 October 1944, Admiral Chester Nimitz and his staff issued a staff study for preliminary planning, which clearly listed the objectives of Operation Detachment. The overriding purpose of the operation was to maintain unremitting military pressure against Japan and to extend American control over the Western Pacific. Three tasks specifically envisioned in the study were the reduction of enemy naval and air strength and industrial facilities in the home islands; the destruction of Japanese naval and air strength in the Bonin Islands, and the capture, occupation, and subsequent defense of Iwo Jima, which was to be developed into an air base. Nimitz's directive declared that "long range bombers should be provided with fighter support at the earliest practicable time", and as such Iwo Jima was "admirably situated as a fighter base for supporting long range bombers."

On 9 October, General Holland Smith received the staff study, accompanied by a directive from Admiral Nimitz ordering the seizure of Iwo Jima. This directive designated specific commanders for the operation. Admiral Raymond A. Spruance, Commander, Fifth Fleet, was placed in charge as Operation Commander, Task Force 50. Under Spruance, Vice Admiral Richmond

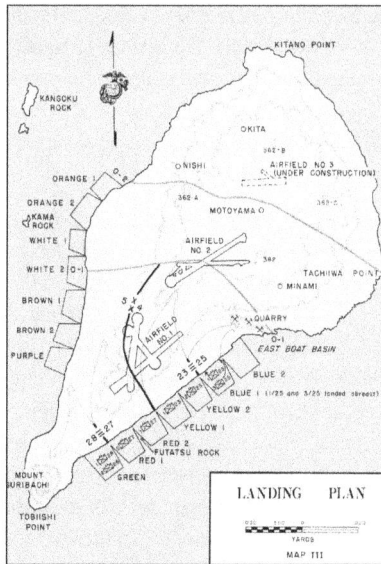

Figure 28: *American landing plan*

Kelly Turner, Commander, Amphibious Forces, Pacific, was to command the Joint Expeditionary Force, Task Force 51. Second in command of the Joint Expeditionary Force was Rear Admiral Harry W. Hill. General Holland Smith was designated Commanding General, Expeditionary Troops, Task Force 56.

It was not accidental that these men were selected to command an operation of such vital importance that it has since become known as "the most classical amphibious assault of recorded history." All of them had shown their mettle in previous engagements. One chronicler of the Iwo Jima operation put it in the following words:

> *'The team assigned to Iwo Jima was superb: the very men who had perfected the amphibious techniques from the Battle of Guadalcanal to the Battle of Guam. Nearly every problem, it was believed, had been met and mastered along the way, from the jungles of Guadalcanal up through the Solomons, and across the Central Pacific from the bloody reefs of Battle of Tarawa to the mountains of the Marianas.'*

Primary plan

The U.S. V Amphibious Corps (VAC) scheme of maneuver for the landings was relatively simple. The 4th and 5th Marine Divisions were to land abreast on the eastern beaches, the 4th on the right and the 5th on the left. When released to VAC, the 3rd Marine Division, as Expeditionary Troops Reserve, was to land over the same beaches to take part in the attack or play a defensive role, whichever was called for. The plan called for a rapid exploitation of the beachhead with an advance in a northeasterly direction to capture the entire island. A regiment of the 5th Marine Division was designated to capture Mount Suribachi in the south. Map of the Plan[94]

The detailed scheme of maneuver for the landings provided for the 28th Marine Regiment of the 5th Marine Division, commanded by Colonel Harry B. Liversedge, to land on the extreme left of the corps on Green 1. On the right of the 28th Marines, the 27th Marine Regiment, under Colonel Thomas A. Wornham, was to attack towards the west coast of the island, then wheel northeastward and seize the O-1 Line. Action by the 27th and 28th Marines was designed to drive the enemy from the commanding heights along the southern portion of Iwo, simultaneously securing the flanks and rear of VAC. As far as the 4th Marine Division was concerned, the 23rd Marine Regiment, commanded by Colonel Walter W. Wensinger, was to go ashore on Yellow 1 and 2 beaches, seize Motoyama Airfield No. 1, then turn to the northeast and seize that part of Motoyama Airfield No. 2 and the O-1 Line within its zone of action. After landing on Blue Beach 1, the 25th Marine Regiment, under Colonel John R. Lanigan, was to assist in the capture of Airfield No. 1, the capture of Blue Beach 2, and the O-1 Line within its zone of action. The 24th Marine Regiment, under Colonel Walter I. Jordan, was to be held in 4th Marine Division reserve during the initial landings. The U.S. 26th Marine Regiment, led by Colonel Chester B. Graham, was to be released from corps reserve on D-Day and prepared to support the 5th Marine Division.

Division artillery was to go ashore on order from the respective division commanders. The 4th Marine Division was to be supported by the 14th Marine Regiment, commanded by Colonel Louis G. DeHaven; Colonel James D. Waller's 13th Marine Regiment was to furnish similar support for the 5th Marine Division.

The operation was to be timed so that at H-Hour 68 Landing Vehicle Tracked (LVT), comprising the first wave, were to hit the beach. These vehicles were to advance inland until they reached the first terrace beyond the high-water mark. The armored amphibians would use their 75 mm howitzers and machine guns to the utmost in an attempt to keep the enemy down, thus giving some measure of protection to succeeding waves of Marines who were most vulnerable to enemy fire at the time they disembarked from their LVTs. Though early versions of the VAC operations plan had called for the Sherman tanks of the 4th and 5th Tank Battalions to be landed at H plus 30, subsequent studies of the beaches made it necessary to adopt a more flexible schedule. The possibility of congestion at the water's edge also contributed to this change in plans.

In the end, the time for bringing the tanks ashore was left to the discretion of the regimental commanders.

Alternate plan

Since there was a possibility of unfavorable surf conditions along the eastern beaches, VAC issued an alternative plan on 8 January 1945, which provided for a landing on the western beaches. However, since predominant northerly or northwesterly winds caused hazardous swells almost continuously along the southwest side of the island, it appeared unlikely that this alternative plan would be put into effect.

Raising the flag on Mt. Suribachi

Raising the Flag on Iwo Jima

Raising the Flag on Iwo Jima is an iconic photograph taken by Joe Rosenthal on February 23, 1945, which depicts six United States Marines raising a U.S. flag atop Mount Suribachi, during the Battle of Iwo Jima, in World War II.

The photograph was first published in Sunday newspapers on February 25, 1945. It was extremely popular and was reprinted in thousands of publications. Later, it became the only photograph to win the Pulitzer Prize for Photography in the same year as its publication, and came to be regarded in the United States as one of the most significant and recognizable images of the war.

Three Marines in the photograph, Sergeant Michael Strank, Corporal Harlon Block (misidentified as Sergeant Hank Hansen until January 1947), and Private First Class Franklin Sousley were killed in action over the next few days. The other three surviving flag-raisers in the photograph were Corporals (then Private First Class) Rene Gagnon, Ira Hayes, and Harold Schultz (misidentified as PhM2c. John Bradley until June 2016).[95] Both men originally misidentified as flag raisers had helped raise a smaller flag about 90 minutes earlier, and were both still on the mountaintop and witnessed – but were not part of – the specific moment of raising the larger flag that was captured in the Pulitzer Prize-winning photo. All men were under the command of Brigadier General Harry B. Liversedge.

The image was later used by Felix de Weldon to sculpt the Marine Corps War Memorial, which was dedicated in 1954 to all Marines who died for their country and is located in Arlington Ridge Park, near the Ord-Weitzel Gate to Arlington National Cemetery and the Netherlands Carillon.

Figure 29: *Mount Suribachi is the dominant ge-*
ographical feature of the island of Iwo Jima

Photo history

On February 19, 1945, the United States invaded Iwo Jima as part of its island-hopping strategy to defeat Japan. Iwo Jima originally was not a target, but the relatively quick fall of the Philippines left the Americans with a longer-than-expected lull prior to the planned invasion of Okinawa. Iwo Jima is located halfway between Japan and the Mariana Islands, where American long-range bombers were based, and was used by the Japanese as an early warning station, radioing warnings of incoming American bombers to the Japanese homeland. The Americans, after capturing the island, weakened the Japanese early warning system, and used it as an emergency landing strip for damaged bombers.[96]

Iwo Jima is a volcanic island, shaped like a trapezoid. Marines on the island described it as "a large, gray pork chop". The island was heavily fortified, and the invading Marines suffered high casualties. Politically, the island is part of the prefecture of Tokyo. It would be the first Japanese homeland soil to be captured by the Americans, and it was a matter of honor for the Japanese to prevent its capture.

The island is dominated by Mount Suribachi, a 546-foot (166 m) dormant volcanic cone at the southern tip of the island. Tactically, the top of Suribachi was one of the most important locations on the island. From that vantage point, the Japanese defenders were able to spot artillery accurately onto the

Americans – particularly the landing beaches. The Japanese fought most of the battle from underground bunkers and pillboxes. It was common for Marines to knock out one pillbox using grenades or a flamethrower, only to come under renewed fire from it a few minutes later, after more Japanese infantry slipped into the pillbox using a tunnel. The American effort concentrated on isolating and capturing Suribachi first, a goal that was achieved on February 23, four days after the battle began. Despite capturing Suribachi, the battle continued to rage for many days, and the island would not be declared "secure" until 31 days later, on March 26.

Two flag-raisings

There were two American flags raised on top of Mount Suribachi, on February 23, 1945. The photograph Rosenthal took was actually of the second flag-raising in which a larger replacement flag was raised by Marines who did not raise the first flag.

Raising the first flag

A U.S. flag was first raised atop Mount Suribachi soon after the mountaintop was captured at around 10:20 on February 23, 1945.

Lieutenant Colonel Chandler Johnson, commander of the 2nd Battalion, 28th Marine Regiment, 5th Marine Division, ordered Marine Captain Dave Severance, commander of Easy Company, 2nd Battalion, 28th Marines, to send a platoon to seize and occupy the crest of Mount Suribachi.[97] First Lieutenant Harold G. Schrier, executive officer of Easy Company, who had replaced the wounded Third Platoon commander, John Keith Wells, volunteered to lead a 40-man combat patrol up the mountain. Lieutenant Colonel Johnson (or 1st Lieutenant George G. Wells, the battalion adjutant, whose job it was to carry the flag) had taken the 54-by-28-inch/140-by-71-centimeter flag from the battalion's transport ship, USS *Missoula*, and handed the flag to Schrier. Johnson said to Schrier, "If you get to the top, put it up." Schrier assembled the patrol at 8 AM to begin the climb up the mountain.

Despite the large numbers of Japanese troops in the immediate vicinity, Schrier's patrol made it to the rim of the crater at about 10:15 am, having come under little or no enemy fire, as the Japanese were being bombarded at the time. The flag was attached by Schrier and two Marines to a Japanese iron water pipe found on top, and the flagstaff was raised and planted by Schrier, assisted by Platoon Sergeant Ernest Thomas and Sergeant Oliver Hansen at about 10:30 am (on February 25, during a CBS press interview aboard the flagship USS *Eldorado* about the flag-raising, Thomas stated that he, Schrier, and Hansen (platoon guide) had actually raised the flag).[98] The

Figure 30: *Raising the First Flag on Iwo Jima by SSgt. Louis R. Lowery, USMC, is the most widely circulated photograph of the first flag flown on Mt. Suribachi (after the flag raising). Left to right: 1st Lt. Harold Schrier (kneeling behind radioman's legs), Pfc. Raymond Jacobs (radioman reassigned from F Company), Sgt. Henry "Hank" Hansen wearing cap, holding flagstaff with left hand, Platoon Sgt. Ernest "Boots" Thomas (seated), Pvt. Phil Ward (holding lower flagstaff with both hands), PhM2c. John Bradley, USN (holding flagstaff with right hand above Ward), Pfc. James Michels (holding M1 Carbine), and Cpl. Charles W. Lindberg (standing above Michels).*

raising of the national colors immediately caused a loud cheering reaction from the Marines, sailors, and coast guardsmen on the beach below and from the men on the ships near the beach. The loud noise made by the servicemen and blasts of the ship horns alerted the Japanese, who up to this point had stayed in their cave bunkers. Schrier and his men near the flagstaff then came under fire from Japanese troops, but the Marines quickly eliminated the threat.Wikipedia:Citation needed Schrier was later awarded the Navy Cross for volunteering to take the patrol up Mount Suribachi and raising the American flag, and a Silver Star Medal for a heroic action in March while in command of D Company, 2/28 Marines on Iwo Jima.

Photographs of the first flag flown on Mount Suribachi were taken by Staff Sergeant Louis R. Lowery of *Leatherneck* magazine, who accompanied the patrol up the mountain, and other photographers.[99],[100] Others involved with the first flag-raising include Corporal Charles W. Lindberg, Privates First Class James Michels and Raymond Jacobs, Private Phil Ward, and Navy corpsman John Bradley[101,102] This flag was too small, however, to be easily seen from the northern side of Mount Suribachi, where heavy fighting would go on for several more days.

The Secretary of the Navy, James Forrestal, had decided the previous night that he wanted to go ashore and witness the final stage of the fight for the mountain. Now, under a stern commitment to take orders from Howlin' Mad Smith, the secretary was churning ashore in the company of the blunt, earthy general. Their boat touched the beach just after the flag went up, and the mood among the high command turned jubilant. Gazing upward, at the red, white, and blue speck, Forrestal remarked to Smith: "Holland, the raising of that flag on Suribachi means a Marine Corps for the next five hundred years".

Forrestal was so taken with fervor of the moment that he decided he wanted the Second Battalion's flag flying on Mt. Suribachi as a souvenir. The news of this wish did not sit well with 2nd Battalion Commander Chandler Johnson, whose temperament was every bit as fiery as Howlin Mad's. "To hell with that!" the colonel spat when the message reached him. The flag belonged to the battalion, as far as Johnson was concerned. He decided to secure it as soon as possible, and dispatched his assistant operations officer, Lieutenant Ted Tuttle, to the beach to obtain a replacement flag. As an afterthought, Johnson called after Tuttle: "And make it a bigger one."[103]

Raising the second flag

The photograph taken by Rosenthal was the second flag-raising on top of Mount Suribachi, on February 23, 1945.

On orders from Colonel Chandler Johnson—passed on by Easy Company's commander, Captain Dave Severance—Sergeant Michael Strank, one of Second Platoon's squad leaders, was to take three members of his rifle squad (Corporal Harlon H. Block and Privates First Class Franklin R. Sousley and Ira H. Hayes) and climb up Mount Suribachi to raise a replacement flag on top; the three took supplies or laid telephone wire on the way up to the top. Severance also dispatched Private First Class Rene A. Gagnon, the battalion runner (messenger) for Easy Company, to the command post for fresh SCR-300 walkie-talkie batteries to take to the top.

Meanwhile, Lieutenant Albert Theodore Tuttle[103] under Johnson's orders, had found a large (96-by-56–inch) flag in nearby Tank Landing Ship USS *LST-779*. He made his way back to the command post and gave it to Johnson.

Johnson, in turn, gave it to Rene Gagnon, with orders to take it up to Schrier on Mount Suribachi and raise it.[104] The official Marine Corps history of the event is that Tuttle received the flag from Navy Ensign Alan Wood of USS *LST-779*, who in turn had received the flag from a supply depot in Pearl Harbor. Severance had confirmed that the second larger flag was in fact provided by Alan Wood even though Wood could not recognize any of the pictures of the 2nd flag raisers as Gagnon.[105] The flag was sewn by Mabel Sauvageau, a worker at the "flag loft" of the Mare Island Naval Shipyard.

First Lieutenant George Greeley Wells, who had been the Second Battalion, 28th Marines adjutant officially in charge of the two American flags flown on Mount Suribachi, stated in the *New York Times* in 1991, that Lieutenant Colonel Johnson ordered him (Wells) to get the second flag, and that he (Wells) sent Rene Gagnon his battalion runner, to the ships on shore for the flag, and that Gagnon returned with a flag and gave it to him (Wells), and that Gagnon took this flag up Mt. Suribachi with a message for Schrier to raise it and send the other flag down with Gagnon. Wells stated that he received the first flag back from Gagnon and secured it at the Marine headquarters command post. Wells also stated that he had handed the first flag to Lieutenant Schrier to take up Mount Suribachi.

The Coast Guard Historian's Office recognizes the claims made by former U.S. Coast Guardsman Quartermaster Robert Resnick, who served aboard the USS *Duval County* at Iwo Jima. "Before he died in November 2004, Resnick said Gagnon came aboard LST-758[106] the morning of February 23 looking for a flag.[107] Resnick said he grabbed a flag from a bunting box and asked permission from his ship's commanding officer Lt. Felix Molenda to donate it.[108] Resnick kept quiet about his participation until 2001."[109]

Rosenthal's photograph

Strank with his three Marines, and Gagnon, reached the top of the mountain around noon without being fired upon. Rosenthal, along with Marine photographers Sergeant Bill Genaust (who was killed in action after the flag-raising) and Private First Class Bob Campbell[110] were climbing Suribachi at this time. On the way up, the trio met Lowery, who had photographed the first flag-raising, coming down. They considered turning around, but Lowery told them that the summit was an excellent vantage point from which to take photographs. The three photographers reached the summit as the Marines were attaching the flag to an old Japanese water pipe.

Rosenthal put his Speed Graphic camera on the ground (set to 1/400 sec shutter speed, with the f-stop between 8 and 11 and Agfa film) so he could pile rocks to stand on for a better vantage point. In doing so, he nearly missed the shot. The Marines began raising the flag. Realizing he was about to miss the action,

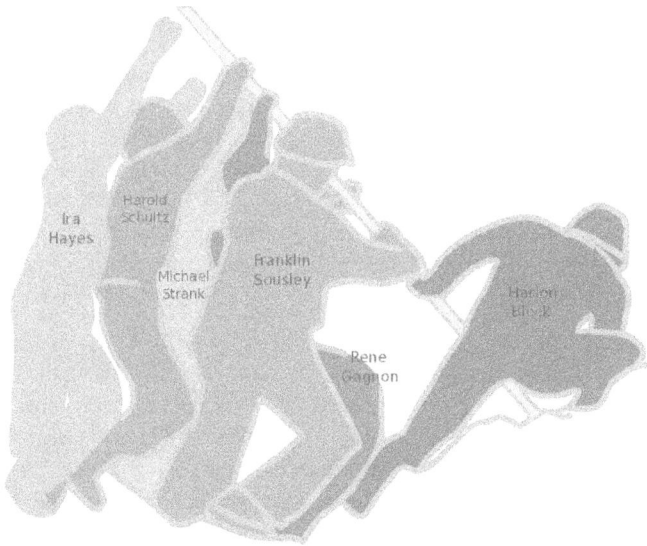

Figure 31: *A diagram of the photograph indicating the six Marines who raised the second flag. Left to right: Ira Hayes, Harold Schultz, Michael Strank (†), Franklin Sousley (†), Rene Gagnon, and Harlon Block (†). "†" = killed in Iwo Jima*

Rosenthal quickly swung his camera up and snapped the photograph without using the viewfinder.[111] Ten years after the flag-raising, Rosenthal wrote:

Out of the corner of my eye, I had seen the men start the flag up. I swung my camera and shot the scene. That is how the picture was taken, and when you take a picture like that, you don't come away saying you got a great shot. You don't know.

Sergeant Genaust, who was standing almost shoulder-to-shoulder with Rosenthal about three feet away, was shooting motion-picture film during the second flag-raising. His film captures the second event at an almost-identical angle to Rosenthal's shot. Of the six flag-raisers in the picture – Ira Hayes, Harold Schultz (identified in June 2016), Michael Strank, Franklin Sousley, Rene Gagnon, and Harlon Block – only Hayes, Gagnon, and Schultz (Navy corpsman John Bradley was incorrectly identified in the Rosenthal flag-raising photo) survived the battle. Strank and Block were killed on March 1, six days after the flag-raising, Strank by a shell, possibly fired from an offshore American destroyer and Block a few hours later by a mortar round. Sousley was shot and killed by a Japanese sniper on March 21, a few days before the island was declared secure.

Publication and staging confusion

Following the flag-raising, Rosenthal sent his film to Guam to be developed and printed. George Tjaden of Hendricks, Minnesota, was likely the technician who printed it. Upon seeing it, Associated Press (AP) photograph editor John Bodkin exclaimed "Here's one for all time!" and immediately transmitted the image to the AP headquarters in New York City at 7:00 am, Eastern War Time.[112] The photograph was quickly picked up off the wire by hundreds of newspapers. It "was distributed by Associated Press within seventeen and one-half hours after Rosenthal shot it—an astonishingly fast turnaround time in those days."

However, the photograph was not without controversy. Following the second flag-raising, Rosenthal had the Marines of Easy Company pose for a group shot, the "gung-ho" shot. A few days after the photograph was taken, Rosenthal—back on Guam—was asked if he had posed the photograph. Thinking the questioner was referring to the 'gung-ho' photograph, he replied "Sure." After that, Robert Sherrod, a *Time-Life* correspondent, told his editors in New York that Rosenthal had staged the flag-raising photograph. *Time*'s radio show, *Time Views the News*, broadcast a report, charging that "Rosenthal climbed Suribachi after the flag had already been planted. ... Like most photographers [he] could not resist reposing his characters in historic fashion." As a result of this report, Rosenthal was repeatedly accused of staging the photograph or covering up the first flag-raising. One *New York Times* book reviewer even went so far as to suggest revoking his Pulitzer Prize. In the following decades, Rosenthal repeatedly and vociferously denied claims that the flag-raising was staged. "I don't think it is in me to do much more of this sort of thing ... I don't know how to get across to anybody what 50 years of constant repetition means." Genaust's film also shows that the flag-raising was not staged.

Mistaken identifications

President Franklin D. Roosevelt, upon seeing Joe Rosenthal's flag-raising photograph, realized the image would make an excellent symbol for the upcoming Seventh War Loan Drive to help pay for the war, and ordered the flag-raisers identified and sent to Washington, D.C. after the fighting on the island ended (March 26, 1945). Using a photographic enlargement, Rene Gagnon identified four other flag-raisers in the photograph besides himself, but refused to identify Ira Hayes as the sixth flag-raiser because Hayes warned him not to.[113] Gagnon revealed Hayes' name only after being brought to Marine Corps headquarters and informed that he was being ordered by the President to reveal the information and that refusing would be a serious crime.

Figure 32: *Joe Rosenthal in 1990*

President Roosevelt died on April 12, 1945. The three surviving second flag-raisers, identified then as Bradley, Gagnon, and Hayes, met President Truman on April 20 at the White House before going on the bond tour which began on May 11 in New York City; Hayes had drinking problems during the tour and was ordered back to his former combat unit in Hawaii on May 24 before the tour ended on July 4 in Washington, D.C. The bond drive was a success, raising $26.3 billion, twice the tour's goal.[114]

Harlon Block and Henry Hansen

Gagnon misidentified Corporal Harlon Block as Sergeant Henry O. "Hank" Hansen in Rosenthal's photo (both were killed in action on March 1). Initially, Bradley concurred with all of Gagnon's identifications. On April 8, 1945, the Marine Corps released the identification of five of the six flag raisers including Hansen rather than Block—Sousley's identity was temporarily withheld pending notification of his family of his death during the battle. Block's mother, Belle Block, refused to accept the official identification, noting that she had "changed so many diapers on that boy's butt, I know it's my boy." Immediately upon his arrival in Washington, D.C. on April 19, Hayes noticed the incorrect identification in the photograph. When he was interviewed about the identities in the photo by the Marine colonel assigned to the flag-raisers and told him that it was definitely Harlon Block and not Hansen in the photograph, the public relations officer then told Hayes that the identifications had already been officially released, and ordered Hayes to keep silent about it[115] (during the investigation, the colonel denied Hayes told him about Block). Block, Sousley, and Hayes were close friends in the same squad of Second Platoon, E Company, while Hansen, who helped raise the first flag, was a member of Third Platoon, E Company.

In 1946, Hayes hitchhiked to Texas and informed Harlon Block's father and mother that Harlon had, in fact, been one of the six flag raisers.[116] Block's mother, Belle, immediately sent a letter that Hayes gave her explaining the error to her congressional representative Milton West. West, in turn, forwarded the letter to Marine Corps Commandant Alexander Vandegrift, who ordered an investigation. John Bradley (formerly in Third Platoon with Hansen), upon being shown the evidence (Hansen, a former Paramarine, wore his large parachutist boots in an exposed manner on Iwo Jima), agreed that it was probably Block and not Hansen.[117] In January 1947, the Marine Corps officially concluded and announced it was Block in the photo and not Hansen.

> *Ira remembered what Rene Gagnon and John Bradley could not have remembered, because they did not join the little cluster until the last moment: that it was Harlon [Block], Mike [Strank], Franklin [Sousley] and [Hayes] who had ascended Suribachi midmorning to lay telephone wire; it was Rene [Gagnon] who had come along with the replacement flag. Hansen had not been part of this action.*[118]

Harold H. Schultz and John Bradley

The Marine Corps made a public announcement on June 23, 2016 stating that Marine Corporal (then Private First Class) Harold Schultz was in the Rosenthal photograph of the flag-raising and Navy Corpsman John Bradley was not (Schultz is now in Franklin Sousley's named position in the photo and Sousley is in Bradley's). Schultz and John Bradley were both present at the first and second flag raising and Sousley only the second raising.

Bradley, who died in 1994, gave few interviews, at times saying that he raised the flag, pitched in to raise the flag, raised the second flag (he also said he was on, and not on, Mount Suribachi when the first flag was raised). Bradley was usually tight-lipped after the war about his wartime experiences, including both flag raisings and did not attend Iwo Jima veterans reunions. He often deflected questions by claiming he had forgotten.[119] During his 47-year marriage, he only talked about it with his wife Betty once, on their first date, and never again afterwards. Within the Bradley family, it was considered a taboo subject, and when they received calls or invitations to speak on certain holidays, they were told to say he was away fishing at his cottage. One of the few interviews he did was in 1985 at the urging of his wife, who had told him to do it for the sake of their grandchildren.[120] Following his death in 1994, his family went to Mount Suribachi on Iwo Jima in 1997 and placed a plaque in memory of John Bradley "Flag Raiser" (made of Wisconsin granite and shaped like that state) at the spot where the flag-raising took place. At the time of Bradley's death, his son James claimed he knew almost nothing from his father about his wartime experiences. James Bradley spent four years interviewing the families of all the flag raisers, and in 2000, published *Flags of Our Fathers*, a definitive book on the flag-raising and its participants.[121] This book inspired a 2006 movie of the same name, directed by Clint Eastwood. Schultz died in 1995.

Photographic comparisons gathered on the first and second flag-raising which were made public in November 2014 by Eric Krelle, a history buff and collector of World War II-era Marine Corps memorabilia, strongly suggested that John Bradley was not one of the actual six flag raisers. According to this research, Franklin Sousley was in the fourth position (left to right) instead of Bradley, and Harold Schultz of Los Angeles (originally from Detroit) was in the second position, previously attributed to Franklin Sousley. Initially, Marine Corps historians and officials and others were not willing to accept these findings. On May 2, 2016, the Marine Corps announced that it was investigating the possibility that Bradley was not one of the flag raisers and Schultz was, a fact they confirmed on June 23, 2016.[122] James Bradley has also subsequently stated that he no longer believes that his father was one of the six men in the Rosenthal photograph.

Legacy

Rosenthal's photograph won the 1945 Pulitzer Prize for Photography, the only photograph to win the prize in the same year it was taken.

News pros were not the only ones greatly impressed by the photo. Navy Captain T.B. Clark was on duty at Patuxent Air Station in Maryland that Saturday when it came humming off the wire in 1945. He studied it for a minute, and then thrust it under the gaze of Navy Petty Officer Felix de Weldon. De Weldon was an Austrian immigrant schooled in European painting and sculpture. De Weldon could not take his eyes off the photo. In its classic triangular lines he recognized similarities with the ancient statues he had studied. He reflexively reached for some sculptor's clay and tools. With the photograph before him he labored through the night. Within 72 hours of the photo's release, he had replicated the six boys pushing a pole, raising a flag.[112] Upon seeing the finished model, the Marine Corps commandant had de Weldon assigned to the Marine

Figure 33: *The flags from the first and second flag-raisings are conserved in the National Museum of the Marine Corps; the second flag, pictured here, was damaged by the high winds at the peak of Suribachi (American flags during World War II had 48 stars, since Alaska and Hawaii were not yet U.S. states).*

Corps until de Weldon was discharged from the navy after the war was over.

Starting in 1951, de Weldon was commissioned to design a memorial to the Marine Corps. It took de Weldon and hundreds of his assistants three years to finish it. Hayes, Gagnon, and Bradley, posed for de Weldon, who used their faces as a model. The three Marine flag raisers who did not survive the battle were sculpted from photographs.

The flag-raising Rosenthal (and Genaust) photographed was the replacement flag/flagstaff for the first flag/flagstaff that was raised on Mount Suribachi on February 23, 1945. There was some resentment from former Marines of the original 40-man patrol that went up Mount Suribachi including by those involved with the first flag-raising, that they did not receive the recognition they deserved. These included: Staff Sgt. Lou Lowery, who took the first photos of the first flag flying over Mt. Suribachi; Charles W. Lindberg, who helped tie the first American flag to the first flagpole on Mount Suribachi (and who was, until his death in June 2007, one of the last living persons depicted in either flag-flying scene), who complained for several years that he helped to raise the flag and "was called a liar and everything else. It was terrible" (because of all the recognition and publicity over and directed to the replacement flag-raisers and that flag-raising); and Raymond Jacobs, photographed with the

Figure 34: *The U.S. Marine Corps War Memorial in Arlington, Virginia*

patrol commander around the base of the first flag flying over Mt. Suribachi, who complained until he died in 2008 that he was still not recognized by the Marine Corps by name as being the radioman in the photo.

The original Rosenthal photograph is currently in the possession of Roy H. Williams, who bought it from the estate of John Faber, the official historian for the National Press Photographers Association, who had received it from Rosenthal. Both flags (from the first and second flag-raisings) are now located in the National Museum of the Marine Corps in Quantico, Virginia.

Ira Hayes, following the war, was plagued with depression brought on by survivor guilt and became an alcoholic. His tragic life and death in 1955 at the age of 32 were memorialized in the 1961 motion picture *The Outsider*, starring Tony Curtis as Hayes, and the folk song "The Ballad of Ira Hayes", written by Peter LaFarge and recorded by Johnny Cash in 1964. Bob Dylan later covered the song, as did Kinky Friedman. According to the song, after the war:

> *Then Ira started drinkin' hard*
>
> *Jail was often his home*
>
> *They'd let him raise the flag and lower it*
>
> *Like you'd throw a dog a bone!*

Figure 35: *U.S. postage stamp, 1945 issue, commemorating the battle of Iwo Jima*

He died drunk early one mornin'

Alone in the land he fought to save

Two inches of water in a lonely ditch

Was a grave for Ira Hayes.

Rene Gagnon, his wife, and his son visited Tokyo and Mount Suribachi on Iwo Jima during the 20th anniversary of the battle of Iwo Jima in 1965.[123] He worked at Delta Air Lines as a ticket agent, opened his own travel agency, and was a maintenance director of an apartment complex in Manchester. He died at work in Manchester in 1979 at the age of 54.[124]

In other media

Rosenthal's photograph has been reproduced in a number of other formats. It appeared on 3.5 million posters for the seventh war bond drive. It has also been reproduced with many unconventional media such as Lego bricks, butter, ice, Etch A Sketch and corn mazes.

The Iwo Jima flag-raising has been depicted in other films including 1949's *Sands of Iwo Jima* (in which the three surviving flag raisers make a cameo appearance at the end of the film) and 1961's *The Outsider*, a biography of Ira Hayes starring Tony Curtis.

In July 1945, the United States Postal Service released a postage stamp bearing the image. The U.S. issued another stamp in 1995 showing the flag-raising as part of its 10-stamp series marking the 50th anniversary of World War II. In 2005, the United States Mint released a commemorative silver dollar bearing the image.

A similar photograph was taken by Thomas E. Franklin of the *Bergen Record* in the immediate aftermath of the September 11 attacks. Officially known as *Ground Zero Spirit*, the photograph is perhaps better known as *Raising the Flag at Ground Zero*, and shows three firefighters raising a U.S. flag in the ruins of the World Trade Center shortly after 5 pm. Painter Jamie Wyeth also painted a related image entitled *September 11th* based on this scene. It illustrates rescue workers raising a flag at Ground Zero. Other iconic photographs frequently compared include *V–J day in Times Square*, *Into the Jaws of Death*, *Raising a flag over the Reichstag*, and the *Raising of the Ink Flag*.

The highly recognizable image is one of the most parodied photographs in history. Anti-war activists in the 1960s altered the flag to bear a peace symbol, as well as several anti-establishment artworks. Edward Kienholz's *Portable War Memorial* in 1968 depicted faceless Marines raising the flag on an outdoor picnic table in a typical American consumerist environment of the 1960s. It was parodied again during the Iran hostage crisis of 1979 to depict the flag being planted into Ayatollah Ruhollah Khomeini's behind. In the early 2000s, to represent gay pride, photographer Ed Freeman shot a photograph for the cover of an issue of *Frontiers* magazine, reenacting the scene with a rainbow flag instead of an American flag.*Time* magazine came under fire in 2008 after altering the image for use on its cover, replacing the American flag with a tree for an issue focused on global warming. The British Airlines Stewards and Stewardesses Association likewise came under criticism in 2010 for a poster depicting employees raising a flag marked "BASSA" at the edge of a runway.

The photograph also received another brief parody in July 2015 in the Syfy television movie *Sharknado 3: Oh Hell No!*, when Fin, April, the President of the United States and a few others hold up the American Flag at the White House in a similar way to the real photograph to impale an incoming shark, with Fin reciting "God bless America."

Bibliography

<templatestyles src="Template:Refbegin/styles.css" />

- Alexander, Joseph H. (1994). *Closing In: Marines in the Seizure of Iwo Jima*. Marines in World War II Commemorative Series. Washington, D.C.: History and Museums Division, Headquarters, U.S. Marine Corps. OCLC 32194668[125].

- Bradley, James (2006) [2000]. *Flags of Our Fathers*. New York: Bantam. ISBN 978-0-553-38415-4.
- Weinberg, Gerhard L. *A World at Arms: A Global History of World War II*. Cambridge; New York: Cambridge University Press. ISBN 978-0-521-55879-2.

Further reading

<templatestyles src="Template:Refbegin/styles.css" />

- Buell, Hal, ed. (2006). *Uncommon Valor, Common Virtue: Iwo Jima and the Photograph that Captured America*. Berkeley, CA: Penguin. ISBN 978-0-425-20980-6.

External links

> Wikimedia Commons has media related to *Raising the Flag on Iwo Jima*.

- *Raising the Flag on Iwo Jima*: The most parodied photo in history?[126]
- Captain Dave Severance talks about the Battle of Iwo Jima and raising the flag[127]
- Chlosta, SSgt Matthew, U.S. Army (July 6, 2007). "JPAC investigation team returns from Iwo Jima (re: William Genaust)"[128]. Joint POW/MIA Accounting Command (JPAC). Archived from the original[129] on November 5, 2011.
- Second World War – Mass on Mount Suribachi[130]

Appendix

References

[1] Taki, THE HISTORY OF BATTLES OF IMPERIAL JAPANESE TANKS http://www3.plala.or.jp/takihome/history2.htm.

[2] B. L. Crumley, "The Marine Corps: Three Centuries of Glory" https//books.google.com, Jan 19, 2013. The total breaks down as follows: 361 artillery pieces of 75 mm caliber or larger, 12 320 mm spigot mortars, 65 medium and light mortars, 33 naval guns, 94 anti-aircraft guns of 75 mm or larger, 200+ anti-aircraft guns of 20 mm or 25 mm, and 69 37 mm or 47 mm anti-tank guns.

[3] John Toland, *The Rising Sun: The Decline and Fall of the Japanese Empire, 1936–1945*, page 669

[4]

[5] John Toland, *Rising Sun: The Decline and Fall of the Japanese Empire 1936–1945*, page 669

[6] Adrian R. Lewis, *The American Culture of War: The History of U.S. Military Force from World War II to Operation Iraqi Freedom*, New York 2007, p. 59

[7] USA, FEC, HistDiv, "Operations in the Central Pacific" – Japanese Studies in World War II (Japanese Monograph No. 48, OCMH), p. 62.; cited in George W. Garand and Truman R. Strobridge (1971). *History of U.S. Marine Corps Operations in World War II* http://www.ibiblio.org/hyperwar/USMC/IV/USMC-IV-VI-1.html. Historical Branch, G-3 Division, Headquarters, U.S. Marine Corps. Vol IV, Part VI, Ch 1.

[8] History of Imperial General Headquarters Army Section, p. 257 http://www.ibiblio.org/hyperwar/Japan/Monos/JM-45/

[9] Wright, *Iwo Jima 1945: The Marines Raise the Flag on Mount Suribachi*, p. 22

[10] Wright, *Iwo Jima 1945: The Marines Raise the Flag on Mount Suribachi*, pp. 22–23

[11] Wright, *Iwo Jima 1945: The Marines Raise the Flag on Mount Suribachi*, pp. 12–13, pp. 80–81

[12] Wright, *Iwo Jima 1945: The Marines Raise the Flag on Mount Suribachi*, p. 23

[13] "Navajo Code Talkers: World War II Fact Sheet" https://www.history.navy.mil/research/library/online-reading-room/title-list-alphabetically/n/code-talkers.html. Naval Historical Center. 1992-09-17. Retrieved 2014-03-12.

[14] Wright, *Iwo Jima 1945: The Marines Raise the Flag on Mount Suribachi*, p. 26

[15] Wright, *Iwo Jima 1945: The Marines Raise the Flag on Mount Suribachi*, pp. 26–27

[16] Leckie, *The Battle for Iwo Jima*, p. 28

[17] Wright, *Iwo Jima 1945: The Marines Raise the Flag on Mount Suribachi*, p. 27

[18] 'We were receiving fire from everywhere' http://www.thestate.com/news/local/military/article14335403.html. *The State*, 2017/12/17.

[19] Leckie, *The Battle for Iwo Jima*, p. 25

[20] Wright, *Iwo Jima 1945: The Marines Raise the Flag on Mount Suribachi*, p. 32

[21] Leckie, *The Battle for Iwo Jima*, pp. 29–31

[22] Wright, *Iwo Jima 1945: The Marines Raise the Flag on Mount Suribachi*, pp. 30–31

[23] Wright, *Iwo Jima 1945: The Marines Raise the Flag on Mount Suribachi*, p. 31

[24] Wright, *Iwo Jima 1945: The Marines Raise the Flag on Mount Suribachi*, p. 33

[25] USMC Statement on Marine Corps Flag Raisers http://www.marines.mil/News/News-Display/Article/810457/usmc-statement-on-iwo-jima-flagraisers/, Office of U.S. Marine Corps Communication, 23 June 2016

[26] https://theamericanwarrior.com/2015/12/06/the-curious-case-of-the-ohio-national-guards-147th-infantry/

[27] See

[28] John Keegan, THE SECOND WORLD WAR, Penguin books, 1989, p.566

[29] John Keegan, p.575

[30] Craven and Cate, 5:559.

[31] Joint War Planning Committee 306/1, "Plan for the Seizure of Rota Island," 25 January 1945.

[32] Reunion of Honor Memorial http://www.traccsofwar.com/article/8286/Reunion-of-Honor-Memorial.htm Retrieved 14 July 2013.

[33] Iwo Jima 50th anniversary US, Japanese vets to meet on Iwo Jima https://www.upi.com/Archives/1995/03/11/Iwo-Jima-50th-anniversary-US-Japanese-vets-to-meet-on-Iwo-Jima/6794794898000/. UPI

[34] See: File:IwoJima Homage Insignia Devices.jpg

[35] Kyodo News, " Map of Iwojima's underground bunkers found in U.S. http://www.japantimes.co.jp/text/nn20120505b2.html", Japan Times, 6 May 2012, p. 2.

[36] //www.worldcat.org/oclc/41157682

[37] //www.worldcat.org/oclc/48215748

[38] //www.worldcat.org/oclc/52071383

[39] //www.worldcat.org/oclc/65978720

[40] http://muse.jhu.edu/login?uri=/journals/journal_of_military_history/v068/68.4burrell.html

[41] //www.worldcat.org/oclc/61499920

[42] //www.worldcat.org/oclc/69104268

[43] //www.worldcat.org/oclc/51968985

[44] //www.worldcat.org/oclc/32971472

[45] //www.worldcat.org/oclc/56015751

[46] https://www.jstor.org/stable/2702942

[47] //www.worldcat.org/oclc/68175700

[48] //www.worldcat.org/oclc/49784806

[49] //www.worldcat.org/oclc/48951047

[50] //www.worldcat.org/oclc/60694955

[51] //www.worldcat.org/oclc/13582622

[52] //www.worldcat.org/oclc/61761637

[53] //www.worldcat.org/oclc/72161745

[54] //www.worldcat.org/oclc/52001277

[55] //www.worldcat.org/oclc/32153036

[56] //www.worldcat.org/oclc/31693687

[57] //www.worldcat.org/oclc/31970164

[58] //www.worldcat.org/oclc/67871973

[59] http://www.nps.gov/wapa/indepth/extContent/usmc/pcn-190-003131-00/index.htm

[60] //www.worldcat.org/oclc/32194668

[61] http://www.ibiblio.org/hyperwar/USMC/USMC-M-IwoJima/index.html

[62] //www.worldcat.org/oclc/28592680

[63] http://www.ibiblio.org/hyperwar/USMC/IV/USMC-IV-VI-1.html

[64] http://www.ibiblio.org/hyperwar/USN/ACTC/index.html

[65] https://web.archive.org/web/20110521010748/http://ibiblio.org/hyperwar/USN/ACTC/index.html

[66] http://www.historyanimated.com/Iwo.html

[67] http://sonicbomb.com/modules.php?name=Downloads&d_op=getit&lid=343

[68] http://www.iwojima.com/

[69] http://ww2db.com/battle_spec.php?battle_id=12

[70] https://web.archive.org/web/20061205095231/http://multimedia.tbo.com/flash/iwojima3d/index.htm

[71] http://multimedia.tbo.com/flash/iwojima3d/index.htm

[72] https://www.denverdonate.com/iwo-jima-john-burgeen.jpg

[73] http://texashistory.unt.edu/young/educators/wwIIjimo/index.shtml

[74] https://web.archive.org/web/20070226225615/http://www.articlemyriad.com/57.htm

[75] http://www.articlemyriad.com/57.htm

[76] http://www.ww2incolor.com/gallery/movies/iwo_jima1

[77] https://web.archive.org/web/20060908083312/http://jscms.jrn.columbia.edu/cns/2005-02-15/lemer-iwojima/

[78] http://jscms.jrn.columbia.edu/cns/2005-02-15/lemer-iwojima/

[79] http://www.lib.utexas.edu/maps/historical/iwo_jima_2003.jpg

[80] https://web.archive.org/web/20090108083553/http://historicalresources.org/2008/09/15/ivo-jima-maps-february-19-1945%E2%80%93march-26-1945/

[81] http://historicalresources.org/2008/09/15/ivo-jima-maps-february-19-1945–march-26-1945/

[82] http://video.google.com/videoplay?docid=-3939121847638029622&q=To+the+Shores+of+Iwo+Jima

[83] http://www.historyofwar.org/articles/battles_iwojima.html

[84] http://www.historynet.com/battle-of-iwo-jima.htm/1

[85] https://web.archive.org/web/20100416171255/http://www.ww2-pictures.com/iwo-jima-pictures.htm

[86] http://www.ww2-pictures.com/iwo-jima-pictures.htm

[87] http://www.history.navy.mil/research/library/online-reading-room/title-list-alphabetically/a/amphibious-operations-capture-iwo-jima.html

[88] https://archive.org/details/VAS_23_Target_Suribachi

[89] https://web.archive.org/web/20090212091322/https://archive.org/details/VAS_23_Target_Suribachi

[90] http://www.awesomestories.com/flicks/flags-fathers/securing-iwo-jima

[91] http://www.iwojimahistory.com

[92] //tools.wmflabs.org/geohack/geohack.php?pagename=Battle_of_Iwo_Jima&params=24_47_N_141_19_E_type:event_region:JP-13

[93] JCS 713/18, "Future Operations in the Pacific", 2 October 1944.

[94] http://www.nps.gov/history/history/online_books/npswapa/extContent/usmc/pcn-190-003131-00/pcn-190-003131-00/images/fig13.jpg

[95] USMC Statement on Marine Corps Flag Raisers http://www.marines.mil/News/News-Display/Article/810457/usmc-statement-on-iwo-jima-flagraisers/, Office of U.S. Marine Corps Communication, 23 June 2016

[96] Weinberg 1999, pp. 866–868.

[97] Bradley 2006, p. 306.

[98] http://ruralfloridaliving.blogspot.com/2012/07/famous-floridian-friday-ernest-ivy.html Rural Florida Living. CBS Radio interview by Dan Pryor with flag raiser Ernest "Boots" Thomas on February 25, 1945 aboard the USS Eldorado (AGC-11): "Three of us actually raised the flag".

[99] Alexander 1994, sec. 4 http://www.nps.gov/history/history/online_books/npswapa/extContent/usmc/pcn-190-003131-00/pcn-190-003131-00/sec4a.htm#flag.

[100] Alexander 1994, cover http://www.nps.gov/history/history/online_books/npswapa/extContent/usmc/pcn-190-003131-00/pcn-190-003131-00/index.htm.

[101] Bradley 2006, p. 205.

[102] http://carol_fus.tripod.com/marines_hero_ray_jacobs.html World War II Stories in Their Own Words

[103] Bradley 2006, p. 207.

[104] Bradley 2006, p. 210.

[105] Battle of Iwo Jima: Alan Wood and the Famous Flag on Mount Suribachi http://www.historynet.com/battle-of-iwo-jima-alan-wood-and-the-famous-flag-on-mount-suribachi.htm HistoryNet, June 12, 2006

[106] LST-758 http://www.navsource.org/archives/10/16/1016075823.jpg

[107] Coast Guard Linked to Iwo Jima http://www.jacksjoint.com/CG%20on%20Iwo%20Jima.htm

[108] USS LST-758 https://www.uscg.mil/history/cutters/USN/LST/LST_758.pdf

[109] USCG Veteran Provided Stars and Stripes for U.S. Marines http://www.uscg.mil/history/weboralhistory/Resnick_Iwo_Jima.asp Silverstein, Judy L.; U.S. Coast Guard.

[110] Farhi, Paul (February 22, 2013) "The Iwo Jima photo and the man who helped save it" The Washington Post, page c1 https://www.washingtonpost.com/lifestyle/style/iwo-jima-photo-and-the-man-who-saw-it-shot/2013/02/21/ee11ab6c-77af-11e2-aa12-e6cf1d31106b_story.html

[111] Bradley 2006, pp. 209–211.

[112] Bradley 2006, p. 220.

[113] Bradley 2006, p. 268.

[114] Bradley 2006, p. 294.

[115] Bradley 2006, p. 275.

[116] Bradley 2006, p. 312.
[117] Bradley 2006, p. 313.
[118] Bradley 2006, p. 274.
[119] Bradley 2006, p. 343.
[120] Bradley 2006, p. 352.
[121] Bradley 2006, p. 5.
[122] http://www.msn.com/en-us/news/us/marines-investigating-claim-about-men-in-iwo-jima-photo/ar-BBsxSdO?ocid=spartandhp
[123] Drake, Hal (February 21, 1965) *Flag raiser's return To Iwo Jima: 'It all seems impossible'* http://www.stripes.com/news/flag-raiser-s-return-to-iwo-jima-it-all-seems-impossible-1.18468 Stars and Stripes
[124] Duckler, Ray (Concord Monitor, May 25, 2014) *Ray Duckler: Son of Marine in iconic photo pays tribute to his father* Retrieved January 4, 2015
[125] //www.worldcat.org/oclc/32194668
[126] http://www.usni.org/iwo-jima-parody-photos
[127] http://feeds.radioamerica.org/rd-bin/rdfeed.mp3?Veterans&cast_id=9849
[128] https://web.archive.org/web/20111105072107/http://www.jpac.pacom.mil/index.php?page=press_center&size=100&ind=0&fldr=PressFeatured&file=IwoJima
[129] http://www.jpac.pacom.mil/index.php?page=press_center&size=100&ind=0&fldr=PressFeatured&file=IwoJima
[130] http://www.worldwar-two.net/events/mass_on_mount_suribachi/

Article Sources and Contributors

The sources listed for each article provide more detailed licensing information including the copyright status, the copyright owner, and the license conditions.

Battle of Iwo Jima *Source:* https://en.wikipedia.org/w/index.php?oldid=852732404 *License:* Creative Commons Attribution-Share Alike 3.0 *Contributors:*   3gocrzy, Absconded Northerner, Alexandervonweimann, Amerijuanican, AntonyZ, Art LaPella, Axeman89, BILB0BAGGINZ, Banedon, BaronNishi, Basilicofresco, Beeline23, Bender235, Benjec, Berean Hunter, Berty688, Beyond My Ken, Bilsonius, Binksternet, Blaylockjam10, Bob-Halford806, BokicaK, Bri, BrianVN, BrxBrx, Bulls123, Byteflush, CAPTAIN RAJU, Calidum, Callanyoloswager, Chapapaman, Chewings72, ClueBot NG, Coltsfan, Count Dude, Cplakidas, DHeyward, DaWulf2013, Dan6hell66, DatGuy, Davidbena, Dcirovic, Demi.holleyervin, Diannaa, DocWatson42, DragonflySixtyseven, El C, Eric Kvaalen, Ericoides, EtherealGate, Evanh12, FoCuSandLeArN, Fortunatestars, Gobonobo, Grandia01, Groyolo, Halomas-terofdoom, Hammersoft, Happyseeu, Hohum, HowlingAngel, Hudson p haeusel, Hungrydog55, Ibadibam, Illegitimate Barrister, IronGargoyle, Italia2006, JSfromILM, Jackfork, Jan Hoellwarth, Jmg38, JoeSmash, Johnscribner, Josve05a, Julietdeltalima, JumpiMaus, JustJust51, KevinMartinCox, KylieTastic, LL Landon P, Leosls, LiberDIO, Lucasjohansson, Magnolia677, Marxist18971, Maryishimotomorris, Maxl, Mboxerwalsh, Mean as custard, Melonkelon, Metavision, Mojoworker, Mr Stephen, Mscuthbert, Mztourist, NFLisAwesome, Neils51, Newzild, Nihiltres, Nihlus1, Oshwah, Pewwer42, Pleiotrop3, Qzd, RandomCritic, Reenem, Rhreimer, RickPer, Rjensen, SWF88, Sannuik12345, Seanpete 11, SemperFi42, Serols, Sheafromme, Shellwood, Simplexity22, Skdndnsjarna, Stesmo, TCMemoire, TeriEmbrey, The Banner, The Pittsburgher, Theinstantmatrix, Tim!, Tobby72, Tony Mach, Trkhoa2016, Trurle, Twin-kleMore, TwoNyce, Valkyrie Red, Vexations, Vloizeau, WW2Historian888, WadeSimMiser, Wavelength, Widr, YahwehSaves, Yamaguchi先生 , Yardism, Yohan Anthony Sunanda, Yuu5757, Zawl, ♡Golf, 191 anonymous edits

Planning for the Battle of Iwo Jima *Source:* https://en.wikipedia.org/w/index.php?oldid=838816140 *License:* Creative Commons Attribution-Share Alike 3.0 *Contributors:*   AntonyZ, Anuoldman, Asperchu, B14709, Barticus88, Bellhalla, Captain Obvious and his crime-fighting dog, Chris the speller, ClueBot NG, Colonies Chris, Davidcannon, Dblecros, Dl2000, Dodgerblue777, El C, Fishicus, Gaius Cornelius, Gavbadger, Gogo Dodo, HanzoHattori, JamesAM, Kill me when i die, Materialscientist, Nick-D, Nightscream, Pen of bushido, Pete Hobbs, Poptropicaman, Reaper Eternal, RekonDog, Renamed user ixgysjijel, Spencer, Strikehold, THEN WHO WAS PHONE?, Vloizeau, WhisperToMe, 30 anonymous edits 1

Raising the Flag on Iwo Jima *Source:* https://en.wikipedia.org/w/index.php?oldid=853240849 *License:* Creative Commons Attribution-Share Alike 3.0 *Contributors:*   83d40m, Acroterion, Agparker, Alistair1978, Alpha19.1, Andy Krtzinger, Andynct, Arjayay, Avoided, BD2412, Bellerophon5685, BillD1, Br'er Rabbit, BreakfastJr, Brucewh, Cabela15, Calidum, Chess, Chrism, Clarityfiend, ClueBot NG, Cléééston, Dank, Dantheman4297, Discospin-ster, DivineAlpha, DocWatson42, Donner60, Doug Coldwell, DouglasCalvert, Dysepsion, East2WestMarine, EdJF, Edmunddantes, El C, Epicgenius, Felicia777, Flyer22 Reborn, Fronticla, Funandtrvl, Garchy, GavinSharp, Generation Great, Gezellig, Gilliam, Gintaras8182, Gobonobo, GreenC, Hmains, Hop on Bananas, InedibleHulk, JMOprof, Jciniello, Jjron, Jmg38, JoeGuru, John of Reading, JohnInDC, Johnsoniensis, Jojhutton, Jrt989, Junes, KMJKWhite, Kablammo, Kaltenmeyer, Kevin Moritz, Klemen Kocjancic, Lizard the Wizard, Lopifalko, Lotje, Messy Thinking, Mike Searson, Mild Bill Hiccup, Mistersierra, Mogism, N0TABENE, Nakedd, Nicklenick, Nightscream, Nihonjoe, Nwbeeson, Oshwah, Pettyfacts, Pharos, Piledhigheranddeeper, Pmaccabe, Prinsgezinde, Qzd, RHodnett, RabitsVinge, Randy Kryn, Raul654, Reenem, RevelationDirect, Rhurst1945, Richard Arthur Norton (1958-), Rockclaw1030, Romeofiveten, Rontrigger, Scanlan, Sir Rhosis, Skizzik, Smalljim, Stithians78, Supersportd, Tages72, ThePangeaGroup, Timrollpickering, Tjohnson2, Tnmbrown, Tpbradbury, Trappist the monk, Val B 1988, Veedub51, VishalB, WFinch, WikiPancake, Worldbruce, YSSYguy, YahwehSaves, Yaush, Yellowdesk, 150 anonymous edits 53

Image Sources, Licenses and Contributors

The sources listed for each image provide more detailed licensing information including the copyright status, the copyright owner, and the license conditions.

Image *Source:* https://en.wikipedia.org/w/index.php?title=File:37mm_Gun_fires_against_cave_positions_at_Iwo_Jima.jpg *License:* Public Domain *Contributors:* User:W.wolny 1
Image *Source:* https://en.wikipedia.org/w/index.php?title=File:Flag_of_the_United_States_(1912-1959).svg *License:* Public Domain *Contributors:* Created by jacobolus using Adobe Illustrator. 1
Image *Source:* https://en.wikipedia.org/w/index.php?title=File:Merchant_flag_of_Japan_(1870).svg *Contributors:* - 1
Image *Source:* https://en.wikipedia.org/w/index.php?title=File:USMC_V_Amphib_Corps.png *License:* Public Domain *Contributors:* Chatsam, Clusternote, Kwasura, Lineagegeek, Smooth O, TonyZ 2
Image *Source:* https://en.wikipedia.org/w/index.php?title=File:Seventh_Air_Force_-_Emblem_(World_War_II).svg *License:* Creative Commons Attribution-ShareAlike 3.0 Unported *Contributors:* historicair 2
Image *Source:* https://en.wikipedia.org/w/index.php?title=File:War_flag_of_the_Imperial_Japanese_Army.svg *License:* Public Domain *Contributors:* Thommy 2
Image *Source:* https://en.wikipedia.org/w/index.php?title=File:Naval_ensign_of_the_Empire_of_Japan.svg *License:* Creative Commons Attribution-ShareAlike 3.0 *Contributors:* Alkari, FDRMRZUSA, Fry1989, Illegitimate Barrister, Morio, NuclearElevator, 2 anonymous edits 2
Image *Source:* https://en.wikipedia.org/w/index.php?title=File:United_States_Fifth_Fleet_insignia_2006.png *License:* Public Domain *Contributors:* Cobatfor, OgreBot 2, Stewi101015 2
Figure 1 *Source:* https://en.wikipedia.org/w/index.php?title=File:Iwo_jima_location_mapSagredo.png *License:* Public Domain *Contributors:* Sagredo 06:09, 31 December 2007 (UTC) 4
Figure 2 *Source:* https://en.wikipedia.org/w/index.php?title=File:Tadamichi_Kuribayashi.jpg *License:* Public Domain *Contributors:* Armagase, Anathema, Get It, Kaba, Kirill Lokshin, PMG, Raul654, SoLando, Sushiya 7
Figure 3 *Source:* https://en.wikipedia.org/w/index.php?title=File:USS_New_York-11.jpg *License:* Public Domain *Contributors:* Benchill, Catsmeat, Denniss, Flamarande~commonswiki, Hohum, Igiveup, Makthorpe, PMG, 1 anonymous edits 9
Figure 4 *Source:* https://en.wikipedia.org/w/index.php?title=File:Harry_Schmidt;USMC-C-Marshalls-p3.jpg *License:* Public Domain *Contributors:* Blackcat, Ebcdic~commonswiki, FieldMarine, Wwoods, Zscout370, ~riley 10
Image *Source:* https://en.wikipedia.org/w/index.php?title=File:Rockey,_Keller_E..jpg *License:* Public Domain *Contributors:* FlickreviewR, Kaganer, Lymantria, Wychmere, 1 anonymous edits 10
Image *Source:* https://en.wikipedia.org/w/index.php?title=File:Clifton_B._Cates.jpg *License:* Public Domain *Contributors:* GrummelJS, Hohum, Howcheng, Lieutcoluseng, Rcbutcher 10
Image *Source:* https://en.wikipedia.org/w/index.php?title=File:Graves_B_Erskine_USMC.jpg *License:* Public Domain *Contributors:* Hungrydog55, Pippobuono 11
Figure 5 *Source:* https://en.wikipedia.org/w/index.php?title=File:Iwo_Jima_-_Landing_Plan.jpg *Contributors:* User:W.wolny 11
Figure 6 *Source:* https://en.wikipedia.org/w/index.php?title=File:Tracked_landing_vehicles_(LVTs)_approach_Iwo_Jima;fig14.jpg *License:* Public Domain *Contributors:* LERK, Morio, PMG, Schaengel89~commonswiki, Shizhao, Wwoods 13
Figure 7 *Source:* https://en.wikipedia.org/w/index.php?title=File:USMC-17446.jpg *License:* Public Domain *Contributors:* 4ing, Magnolia677, OgreBot 2, Reguyla 14
Figure 8 *Source:* https://en.wikipedia.org/w/index.php?title=File:Marines_burrow_in_the_volcanic_sand_on_the_beach_of_Iwo_Jima.jpg *License:* Public Domain *Contributors:* User:W.wolny 14
Figure 9 *Source:* https://en.wikipedia.org/w/index.php?title=File:Marines_with_LVT(A)-5_in_Iwo_Jima_1945.jpg *License:* Public Domain *Contributors:* Taken by a Fifth Marine Division photographer. 16
Figure 10 *Source:* https://en.wikipedia.org/w/index.php?title=File:Stars_and_Stripes_on_Mount_Suribachi_(Iwo_Jima).jpg *Contributors:* Photo 26-G-4140, U.S. Department of Transportation. U.S. Coast Guard. Office of Public and International Affairs 20
Figure 11 *Source:* https://en.wikipedia.org/w/index.php?title=File:Iwo-Jima-3c.jpg *License:* Public Domain *Contributors:* US Post Office, Bureau of Engraving and Printing 20
Figure 12 *Source:* https://en.wikipedia.org/w/index.php?title=File:Iwo_Jima_Tunnels.JPG *License:* Public Domain *Contributors:* US Navy .. 22
Figure 13 *Source:* https://en.wikipedia.org/w/index.php?title=File:Browning_M1917_Marine_Iwo_Jima_fixed.jpg *License:* Public Domain *Contributors:* USMC 23
Figure 14 *Source:* https://en.wikipedia.org/w/index.php?title=File:Ronson_flame_tank_Iwo_Jima.jpg *License:* Public Domain *Contributors:* Life Magazine photographer Mark Kauffman (1922-1994) (Official USMC photograph) 24
Figure 15 *Source:* https://en.wikipedia.org/w/index.php?title=File:Flamethrower-iwo-jima-194502.jpg *License:* Public Domain *Contributors:* Avron, Bukvoed, Catsmeat, Ingolfson, KMJKWhite, Manxruler, PMG, Saibo 26
Figure 16 *Source:* https://en.wikipedia.org/w/index.php?title=File:Captured_Japanese_flag_on_Iwo_Jima.jpg *License:* Public Domain *Contributors:* User:W.wolny 27
Figure 17 *Source:* https://en.wikipedia.org/w/index.php?title=File:Lieutenant_Wade_discusses_overall_importance_of_target_at_pre-invasion_briefing_HD-SN-99-02874.jpg *License:* Public Domain *Contributors:* De728631, Fæ 28
Figure 18 *Source:* https://en.wikipedia.org/w/index.php?title=File:American_supplies_being_landed_at_Iwo_Jima.JPEG *Contributors:* PhoM2c, Paul Queenan, USCG 28
Figure 19 *Source:* https://en.wikipedia.org/w/index.php?title=File:24th_marines_wwii_iwo_jima.jpg *License:* Public Domain *Contributors:* FieldMarine, Hdtychse, Howard61313 29
Figure 20 *Source:* https://en.wikipedia.org/w/index.php?title=File:Harry_Truman_congratulates_Hershel_Williams_on_being_awarded_the_Medal_of_Honor.jpg *License:* Public Domain *Contributors:* Official USMC Photograph 31
Figure 21 *Source:* https://en.wikipedia.org/w/index.php?title=File:USMC_War_Memorial_Night.jpg *License:* Public Domain *Contributors:* Catie Drew 32
Figure 22 *Source:* https://en.wikipedia.org/w/index.php?title=File:MemorialonMtSuribachi.jpg *License:* Public Domain *Contributors:* U.S. Navy photo by Lt. Bill EvansFirstly cropped by Durin on the English Wikipedia (MemorialonMtSuribachi.jpg), uploaded 32
Figure 23 *Source:* https://en.wikipedia.org/w/index.php?title=File:60th_Anniversary_reunion_at_Iwo_Jima.jpg *License:* Public Domain *Contributors:* U.S. National Park Service 33
Image *Source:* https://en.wikipedia.org/w/index.php?title=File:Commons-logo.svg *License:* logo *Contributors:* Anomie, Callanecc, CambridgeBay-Weather, Jo-Jo Eumerus, RHaworth 37
Figure 24 *Source:* https://en.wikipedia.org/w/index.php?title=File:View_of_Iwo_Landing_Beach_from_top_of_Suribachi.jpg *License:* Public Domain *Contributors:* Athaenara, BotMultichill, Fallschirmjäger, File Upload Bot (Magnus Manske), Foroa, OgreBot 2, Penarc 40
Figure 25 *Source:* https://en.wikipedia.org/w/index.php?title=File:Iwo_Jima_Tunnels.JPG *License:* Public Domain *Contributors:* US Navy ... 41
Figure 26 *Source:* https://en.wikipedia.org/w/index.php?title=File:Japanese_120mm_Gun_at_Iwo_Jima.jpg *Contributors:* User:W.wolny ... 44
Figure 27 *Source:* https://en.wikipedia.org/w/index.php?title=File:Lieutenant_General_Holland_M._Smith.jpg *License:* Public Domain *Contributors:* User:W.wolny ... 47
Figure 28 *Source:* https://en.wikipedia.org/w/index.php?title=File:Iwo_Jima_-_Landing_Plan.jpg *Contributors:* User:W.wolny 49
Figure 29 *Source:* https://en.wikipedia.org/w/index.php?title=File:Iwo_Jima_Suribachi_DN-SD-03-11845.JPEG *License:* Public Domain *Contributors:* Phan Lee McCaskill, USN 54
Figure 30 *Source:* https://en.wikipedia.org/w/index.php?title=File:First_Iwo_Jima_Flag_Raising.jpg *License:* Public Domain *Contributors:* Staff Sergeant Louis R. Lowery, USMC, staff photographer for "Leatherneck" magazine 56
Figure 31 *Source:* https://en.wikipedia.org/w/index.php?title=File:Raising_the_Flag_outline.svg *License:* Creative Commons Attribution-Sharealike 3.0 *Contributors:* User:Aeoris 59
Figure 32 *Source:* https://en.wikipedia.org/w/index.php?title=File:Joerosenthal1990.jpg *Contributors:* User:Edmunddantes 61
Figure 33 *Source:* https://en.wikipedia.org/w/index.php?title=File:IwoJimaFlag.jpg *License:* Creative Commons Attribution-ShareAlike 3.0 Unported *Contributors:* 17Drew~commonswiki, FieldMarine, KTo288, Morio, Pierre cb, Smooth O, SteveHopson, Trixt, ŠJů, 1 anonymous edits 64
Figure 34 *Source:* https://en.wikipedia.org/w/index.php?title=File:USMC_War_Memorial_Night.jpg *License:* Public Domain *Contributors:* Catie Drew 65
Figure 35 *Source:* https://en.wikipedia.org/w/index.php?title=File:3c-Iwo_Jima.jpg *License:* Public Domain *Contributors:* US Post Office 66

License

Index

www.ingramcontent.com/pod-product-compliance
Lightning Source LLC
Chambersburg PA
CBHW031539040426
42445CB00010B/612